WITHDRAWN

GALATA AND PERA AND THE BRIDGE OF BOATS CONNECTING WITH STAMBOUL, CONSTANTINOPLE

DAYBREAK IN TURKEY

BY

JAMES L. BARTON, D.D.

Secretary of the American Board

AUTHOR OF

"THE MISSIONARY AND HIS CRITICS," "THE UNFINISHED TASK OF THE CHRISTIAN CHURCH," ETC.

SECOND EDITION

BOSTON
THE PILGRIM PRESS
NEW YORK   CHICAGO

Copyright, 1908
By James L. Barton

Seventh Thousand

DR
572
B2

THE · PLIMPTON · PRESS
NORWOOD MASS · U · S · A

To the revered memory of that noble company of men and women of all races and creeds who have toiled and sacrificed and died that Turkey might be free, this volume is dedicated.

FOREWORD

THIS book was not written in order to catch popular favor at this time of revolution in the Ottoman empire. All except the concluding chapter was prepared some time before the 24th of July, 1908, and the entire work was at that time nearly ready for the press. Much of the material had been used in the Hyde Lecture Course at Andover Seminary and in the Alden Lecture Course at the Chicago Theological Seminary. The chapter, "Turkey and the Constitution," was written since the overthrow of the old régime, and appeared as an article in *The Outlook* in September, 1908. The book does not pretend to be an exhaustive study of the Turkish empire and its problems. Such a work would necessarily be encyclopedic in its size and scope.

The purpose from the beginning has been briefly and clearly to set forth the various historical, religious, racial, material, and national questions having so vital a bearing upon all Turkish matters, and which now reveal the forces that have had so much to do in changing Turkey from an absolute monarchy into a constitutional and representative government. Reformations have never come by accident, and this moral and political revolution in Turkey, the most sweeping of all, is no exception. To one who traces the entrance and

FOREWORD

development in the Ottoman empire during the last century, of reformative ideas in the religious, intellectual, and social life of the people, the present almost bloodless revolution presents no mysteries. It is but the fruit of the seeds of intelligence, of righteousness, and of holy ambition, sown in good soil and now bearing fruit after their kind.

J. L. B.

Boston, December, 1908.

INTRODUCTION

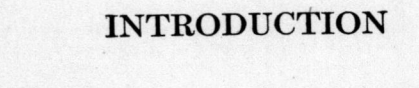

ONE of the obstacles which lie in the path of the European when he wants to arrive at the true opinion of the Oriental is that the European, especially if he be an official, is almost always in a hurry. If, he thinks, the Oriental has anything to say to me, why does he not say it and go away? I am quite prepared to listen most attentively, but my time is valuable and I have a quantity of other business to do; I must, therefore, really ask him to come to the point at once. This frame of mind is quite fatal if one wishes to arrive at the truth. In order to attain this object, the Oriental must be allowed to tell his story and put forward his ideas in his own way; and his own way is generally a lengthy, circuitous, and very involved way. But if any one has the patience to listen, he will sometimes be amply rewarded for his pains.

I once asked a high Moslem authority how he reconciled the fact that an apostate could now no longer be executed with the alleged immutability of the Sacred Law. The casuistry of his reply would have done honor to a Spanish Inquisitor. The Kadi, he said, does not recognise any change in the Law. He would, in the case of an apostate, pronounce sentence of death according to the Law, but it was for the secular authorities to carry out the sentence. If they failed in their duty, the sin of disobeying the Law would lie on their heads. Cases of apostasy are very rare, but during my tenure of office in Egypt, I had to interfere once or twice to protect from maltreatment Moslems who had been converted to Christianity by the American missionaries.

The reasons why Islam as a social system has been a complete failure are manifold.

First and foremost, Islam keeps women in a position of marked inferiority. In the second place, Islam, speaking not so much through the Koran as through the traditions which cluster round the Koran, crystallises religion and law into one inseparable and immutable whole, with the result that all elasticity is taken away from the social system. If to this day an Egyptian goes to law over a question of testamentary succession, his case is decided according to the antique principles which were laid down as applicable to the primitive society of the Arabian Peninsula in the seventh century. — LORD CROMER in "Modern Egypt."

INTRODUCTION

NO other country is so hard to understand, in its political, intellectual, industrial, and religious conditions, as the Turkish empire. This difficulty is augmented by the fact that no one of these conditions can be even measurably understood without a knowledge of the others. It is this which accounts for the widely divergent opinions expressed by casual travelers, and makes well-nigh impossible an explanation of Turkish phenomena to one who as yet knows nothing of the country and people, of actual conditions and the reasons for them.

Turkey differs in almost every respect from all other countries. Its government has no parallel either in fundamental principles of organization or in methods of administration. It is unique in its religious beliefs, unexampled in its educational conditions, and incalculable in its dealings with moral and religious questions. We entertain notions of right and wrong that are generally accepted by the nations of Christendom as well as by many others not so classed. These conceptions constitute the fundamental principles of international usage and form the basis for what we call International Law. To conclude, however, that these generally accepted principles will command recognition in Turkey as the basis for its international relations is to invite disappointment. Turkey recognizes no such law as having force in its empire.

In the dealings of one nation with another it is customary to regard the verbal pledge of a sovereign or cabinet minister as worthy of credence, and a basis for negotiations, at least, if not for final adjustment. This notion

INTRODUCTION

must be laid aside as purely academic and visionary, in dealing with Turkey.

In view of such facts, it is plain that no phase of Turkish life or affairs can be clearly understood without considerable knowledge of the country and its history, the government and its administrative processes, the diversified religions of its people, and their interdependence. Such a knowledge is especially necessary to anything like an intelligent comprehension of the problems and methods of mission work in the empire of Turkey.

All the chapters of this book except the last were written as they stand, some months before the promulgation of the Constitution on July 24, 1908. A reading of this manuscript suggests no alterations in the light of recent facts except the addition of a statement of the immediate events that led to the overthrow of the old régime and the inauguration of the new order. Obviously only the transitions can be recorded here. The new constitutional government has yet to demonstrate its stability.

CONTENTS

Chapter		Page
I.	The Country	13
II.	Its Resources	21
III.	History and Government	29
IV.	The Sultan, the Heart of Turkey	39
V.	Race Questions and Some of the Races	49
VI.	The Armenians	63
VII.	Moslem Peoples	71
VIII.	Turkey and the West	83
IX.	A Strategic Missionary Center	91
X.	Social, Moral and Religious Conditions	99
XI.	Christianity and Islam	111
XII.	Early Pioneering and Explorations	117
XIII.	Established Centers	135
XIV.	Beginnings in Reform	147
XV.	Leaders, Methods, and Anathemas	155
XVI.	Results	169
XVII.	Intellectual Renaissance	179
XVIII.	The Printing-Press	195

CONTENTS

Chapter		Page
XIX.	Modern Medicine	205
XX.	Standing of Missionaries	211
XXI.	Completed Work	221
XXII.	Industrial and Religious Changes	231
XXIII.	American Rights	239
XXIV.	Religious Toleration	247
XXV.	The Macedonian Question	259
XXVI.	General Political Situation	265
XXVII.	Constitutional Government	273
XXVIII.	The Constitution Vindicated	289
Index		301

ILLUSTRATIONS

Galata and Pera and the bridge of boats connecting with Stamboul, Constantinople . . . . *Frontispiece*

A group of official Turks in prayer for the Sultan upon his birthday 42

A Koordish chief of Southern Koordistan 68

An Armenian Ecclesiastic 68

A mountain village in Eastern Turkey 94

The Bosporus, Constantinople 94

Robert College, Constantinople 184

Syrian Protestant College, Beirut, Syria 184

A class of native students, graduates from the American College for Girls, Constantinople 224

The illustration on the front cover shows the ruins of the Arch of Constantine, Salonica, Macedonia.

THE COUNTRY

In attempting to understand this motley field, two principles of the empire must always be kept in mind. One is the Mohammedan principle, which allows non-idolatrous peoples to retain their religion on payment of a poll-tax, at the same time freeing them from military duty. The other is the Turkish principle, which allows different nationalities to remain distinct, but requires them to be represented before the sultan by a political or religious head. There is no assimilating power tending to unify these many races and religions, like that of the British, or even the Mughals, in India. The consequence is that all these separate units form a conglomerate state, binding religions and nationalities together in a repellent contact ready to fly apart into fragments the moment the external fettering bond snaps. — EDWARD A. LAWRENCE in "Modern Missions in the East."

DAYBREAK IN TURKEY

I. THE COUNTRY

WHEN the Turks laid siege to Vienna in 1529 it was the period of their greatest prosperity. If at that time the entire Ottoman empire had been enclosed by a modest wall it would have taken a large army of workmen from that day to the present to tear down the old boundaries and reerect them upon the new lines. A most interesting feature of this constant change is that it has been almost uniformly a decrease in the area of the empire. At that time it was the most powerful realm in the world. It included all the states bordering upon the Mediterranean except Spain, France, Italy, and Morocco, the entire Black Sea coast, and nearly all that of the Red Sea, as well as the lower Danube district. Gradually province after province and state after state have slipped from the grasp of the sultan. The decline became decided in 1606 beginning with the treaties of the Sitavorok. With the treaty of Carlowitz in 1699 it amounted to actual dismemberment. The epithet, "The sick man of the East," was applied to the sultan, after this loss of prestige from which he never recovered. The retrograde movement continued through the seventeenth century. While the Ottoman empire had been the object of extreme fear upon the part of the nations of Europe up to the beginning of that century, each of them vying with the rest in seeking the favor and good-will of the reigning sultan, at the beginning of the eighteenth century Turkey had reached a point where it was protected by its relative weakness. It no longer inspired fear in the hearts of European rulers, while its impotency and the mutual antagonism of its subject non-Moslem races rendered aggressive national action practically impossible. Parts of its territory became wholly lost, like the Danube provinces, the Caucasus and Tunis, while other sections became semi-independent like Bulgaria, Cyprus, Crete, and Egypt.

The Turkish empire may now be defined as covering Macedonia in Europe, extending west to Greece, northward to include Albania, Bulgaria, and Adrianople, — all of Asia Minor to the Russian and Persian borders upon the east, Syria and Arabia, with two small sections of Africa and a few islands in the Mediterranean. It exercises no actual control of Egypt, while its hold upon parts of Arabia is constantly contested by the people themselves.

The size and population of territory under direct control of Turkey are:

Europe	65,350 sq. miles;	6,130,200	inhabitants
Asia	693,610 " "	16,898,700	"
Africa	398,900 " "	1,000,000	"
	1,157,860	24,028,900	

Under indirect control:

Bulgaria and Eastern Roumelia	37,200 sq. miles;	3,744,300	inhabitants
Bosnia, etc.	19,800 " "	1,591,100	"
Crete	3,330 " "	310,400	"
Cyprus	3,710 " "	237,000	"
Samos	180 " "	54,840	"
Egypt	400,000 " "	9,820,700	"
	464,220 " "	15,758,340	"

This makes a total area covered by both the immediate and quasi possessions of the sultan 1,622,080 square miles,

THE COUNTRY

with a population of 39,787,240. These are the figures given by the Statesman's Year-Book, the best attainable authority upon the subject; but even these must be taken largely as estimates and not as the results of a careful and reliable census, — something that never takes place in Turkey.

It may be said, therefore, that at the present time the sultan of Turkey actually rules over only Constantinople, the Macedonian provinces in Europe and Asia Minor to the borders of Russia and Persia, extending south through Syria and into Arabia. This includes an area of about 704,000 square miles, and a population of about 23,500,000.

These countries directly and indirectly governed by the Turkish empire command the interest of the Biblical, classical, and historical student beyond any other part of the earth. No other land possesses so many antiquities of such priceless worth. Turkey is the stage upon which many of the best-known characters of literature and history have lived and acted. It is the battle-field where, for more than thirty-five centuries, contending civilizations and hostile religions, under ambitious leadership, have met in bloody conflict. There is hardly a section of it that has not been connected directly with some well-known historical personage or race or that has not given the setting to some event of world-wide renown. This is true from Salonica on the Ægean Sea to Persia upon the east, and from Trebizond upon the Black Sea at the north to Aden at the southern point of Arabia. The ruins of massive castles and fortresses, moats and walled cities, that tell of former strength, of pride and of conflict, are found in almost every part of the empire. Inscriptions in many languages adorn the cliffs or are built into walls now crumbling to ruin.

Fragments of ancient roads with arches of bridges and of aqueducts still standing, as old as our Christian era, tell of the engineering skill of the early possessors of the land.

In the soil thrown up beneath one's feet are found gold, silver, bronze, and copper coins, with dates varying from six hundred years before our Christian era to the coin of the present ruler of the realm.

The ancient city of the Trojans, for ten years defended by Priam against the finally successful assaults of Agamemnon and his Greeks, was upon what is now Turkish soil. Many of the scenes pictured in the Iliad and the Odyssey have their staging in what is modern Turkey. Assyria and Babylon and Nineveh there arose into prominence, wielded their power, and passed into ruin. Darius and Xerxes crossed and recrossed this country; and Cyrus met his great defeat and Xenophon made his immortal retreat and all within Turkey. Alexander the Great, born in Macedonia, conducted many of his brilliant campaigns, fought with Darius and defeated him, occupied Sidon and annexed Babylon and Nineveh to the throne of Greece, and died in Babylon while planning the conquest of Arabia; all in territory now subject to Sultan Hamid II.

At the time of Christ much of Asia Minor was a Roman province. Ruins of Roman roads and Roman bridges, in many parts of the country, extend to the northern borders of Mesopotamia, while Roman coins and Latin inscriptions are too common to attract special attention. It is safe to say that there is no other part of the world which presents so much of permanent interest to the student of classic literature and life as the territory now covered by the Turkish empire.

The same is true in no less striking measure of the litera-

THE COUNTRY

ture and life recorded in the Bible. Probably all Old Testament history, except that part which was enacted in Egypt, belongs to the geography of Turkey; and Egypt, until recent years, was a part of that empire. The Tigris and Euphrates rivers rise and flow throughout their length upon Turkish soil. Chaldea, Haran, Mt. Moriah, Sinai, the Wilderness, Nineveh, and the Promised Land are a part of the present Moslem empire. Turkey includes the land of the prophets and kings of Israel, and from what is to-day her domain the Hebrew poets sang; there, too, the temples were built, the chosen race was scattered, enslaved, and restored.

Except for one brief sojourn of our Lord in Egypt, his entire life was passed on what is now Turkish territory. With few exceptions the apostles lived and labored and wrote and died in regions now ruled over by the sultan of Turkey. The great foreign missionary, Paul, spent but little time outside this country, while the site of the seven churches of the Apocalypse is in Turkish territory. The most of our Christian Scriptures were written in the same country, passing from there to the west.

The land of Turkey may well be called the cradle of classic and Biblical literature of the Jewish and Christian religions as well as that of Islam. All this, however, be it not forgotten, refers only to the territory covered to-day by the Turkish empire and not at all to the empire itself.

ITS RESOURCES

THE dominion of the Ottoman clan, which should have been a mere passing phenomenon, like the similar dominion of another Tartar clan in Russia, owes its continuance, as we read its history, to three causes, two of them intellectual. The first is the extraordinary, indeed the absolutely unrivalled force displayed through ages by the descendants of Othman, the Tartar chief from Khorassan. The old line, "An Amurath, an Amurath succeeds," has been substantially true. Sprung originally from a stock welded into iron by the endless strife of the great Asiatic desert, mating always with women picked for some separate charm either of beauty or captivation, the sultans, with the rarest exceptions, have been personages, great soldiers, great statesmen, or great tyrants. Mahmoud the destroyer of the Janissaries, who only died in 1839 — that is, while men still middle-aged were alive — was the equal in all but success of Amurath I, who organized, though he did not invent, that terrible institution; and even the present sultan, in many ways so feeble, is no Romulus Augustulus, no connoisseur in poultry, but a timid Louis XI, who overmatches Russians and Greeks in craft, who terrifies men like his Ottoman Pashas, and who is obeyed with trembling by the most distant servant of his throne. The terrible emir of Afghanistan, whose satraps, while ruling provinces and armies, open his letters "white in the lips with fear," is not regarded with more slavish awe than Abdul Hamid, the recluse who watches always in his palace against assassination or mutiny. We have only to remember what the Hohenzollerns have been to Prussia, to understand what the family of Othman, defended as they have been against revolution by the Mussulman belief that "when Othman falls Islam falls," has been to a fighting clan. — MEREDITH TOWNSEND in "Asia and Europe."

II. ITS RESOURCES

THE countries under Turkish rule are lands of real resource, and yet a superficial view of the greater part of the Turkish empire gives one the impression of extreme poverty. Throughout most of the country the hills have been denuded of timber, and trees are found only where they are cultivated. There are still some forest lands bordering on the southern shores of the Black Sea, especially towards the east. In Armenia, the region in which the Tigris and Euphrates rivers have their rise, even the roots of the scrub-oaks that grow upon the low mountains and high plateaux are dug up for fuel. The crops, in large part, are raised by the most primitive methods of irrigation, although in the western part of Asia Minor, as well as in other sections, considerable high land crops are produced. These are uncertain, owing to frequent failure of the rains. There are other large sections, like the plains to the north of the modern city of Diarbekr — the ancient city of Amida upon the banks of the Tigris — where for lack of surface water a large area of the richest arable land lies waste, except as flocks and herds roam over it during the rainy season in the spring.

Yet there are few countries in the world that can boast of richer or more productive soil than can Turkey. There are desert regions in Arabia, but these are not as extensive as we have been wont to suppose. Turkey exports more foodstuffs than she imports, although her agricultural resources are but slightly developed. The method of farming is entirely antiquated, the same primitive plow being in constant use to-day that was employed by Abraham in the fields of Haran. In spite of this fact, wheat of excellent quality, barley, rice, millet, cotton, tobacco, the opium poppy, and almost all kinds of vegetables, as well as grapes, plums, cherries, olives, quinces, oranges, lemons, figs, and pomegranates are produced in great abundance. The mulberry-tree flourishes in many regions. Sheep, goats, and a stunted breed of cattle and the water-buffalo, donkeys and horses thrive in most parts of the country, while as beasts of burden the camel and mule are found in all sections of Asiatic Turkey.

The country is also rich in minerals, but the mines are undeveloped. By the laws of the land, all minerals belong to the government, hence no private mining enterprises are permitted. Coal is found in many parts of the country, but being a mineral, by government classification, it cannot be mined except officially. Copper, silver, and lead abound, but the few mines worked by the government have not been paying enterprises except to the official in charge.

In a word, Turkey is naturally a rich country, with boundless resources now largely undeveloped, with undreamed-of possibilities of increased production under modern methods of agriculture and mining. It is probably true that the empire includes some of the very richest land and ore deposits in the world.

Exportation from Turkey is limited to the coast borders and to the proximity of the few railways that exist. Railroads are confined to the European district and the eastern section of Asia Minor, with a short line reaching to Tarsus and Adana from Mersin and one from Joppa up to Jerusalem. New lines are under construction intending to connect Damascus with Mecca. Railroads cannot long be kept out of the interior of the country. There are but few made wagon roads, nearly all of which have been constructed

ITS RESOURCES

since the Crimean war in 1854. One of the most noted of these few roads over which wheeled vehicles can pass extends from Samsoun upon the middle southern coast of the Black Sea, through Marsovan, Tokat, Amasia, Sivas, Malatia, Harpoot, and Diarbekr, ending at Mardin, a distance of nearly six hundred miles. Some of the bridges planned were never built, and many were washed away soon after construction. Another highway of a similar nature extends from Trebizond to Erzerum. Others have been recently built in Northern Syria. These roads never fail to be in poor repair. But the ordinary roads are worse, being in all parts of the empire mere bridle-paths, often worn deep in the solid rock by the hoof-beats of the caravans of fifty centuries.

These conditions necessitate in the interior the transportation of all freight by horse or camel, thus discouraging commerce and trade, increasing the price of imports and making export practically impossible. This explains why a famine may prevail in one part of the country when at the same time, less than three hundred miles away, the crops are abundant. A good system of railroads would revolutionize everything. There is an abundance of foreign capital ready to construct such roads. Some fifteen years ago the plan was practically consummated to build a railroad from Samsoun through Asia Minor down across northern Mesopotamia to Bagdad. At the last moment the plan was thwarted by the sultan himself. In conversation upon this matter with an intelligent Mohammedan official who had been educated in England and France, the writer asked him if he did not understand that such a road would bring much wealth into the country, and at the same time develop far more wealth in the country itself. He was asked if he had studied the railroads of America and Europe and observed the great value they were in every way in those countries. His reply was characteristic. It was in substance, " I know well that all that you say of the value of railroads to a country is true. You have not overstated it. At the same time I know, and so does my master, the sultan, that every dollar of foreign capital that comes into this country under concessions as an investment, curtails by so much the authority of the sultan in his own domains. Such capital always brings with it foreign protection. If his imperial majesty should change his mind, as he has full right to do at any time, in regard to any of these concessions, he is at once confronted by the protests of that country to which the capital belongs, demanding that he adhere to the original agreement or pay damages. The ruler of the Ottoman empire will never willingly submit to such humiliation. When railroads are built through Turkey, his majesty will construct them himself."

This explains why foreign capital is not building railroads, developing mines, and constructing factories in that country. It explains why, in this respect, Turkey is still in the depths of the dark ages.

The telegraph system of the country is entirely in the hands of the government and reaches every city of any considerable size. This became necessary to the sultan in order to carry on the processes of government. Telegrams are carefully censored; cipher despatches, when known to be such, are not accepted except from ambassadors and from foreign powers to their chief at the Porte, or vice versa. The postal system is antiquated, irregular, and uncertain, reaching only the large towns upon the limited cross-country routes. Telephones are strictly prohibited.

In Constantinople and in several of the port cities like

ITS RESOURCES

Smyrna, Trebizond, etc., there are foreign post-offices supported and conducted by foreign countries and using foreign stamps. These became necessary because of the unreliability of the Turkish offices. The local government has made several attempts to abolish the sale and use of foreign postage-stamps in the country, but has failed of accomplishing it because the representatives of the leading foreign powers are unwilling to trust their mail to Turkish supervision and control.

HISTORY AND GOVERNMENT

EVEN now, when we all talk of the Turkish empire as moribund, it is doubtful if it will perish under any decay from within. The subject races do not grow stronger, as witness recent scenes in Armenia, where a single tribe, with only tolerance from the sultan, keeps a whole people in agonies of fear. The Arabs, full-blooded and half-caste, who might succeed in insurrection, find the strength of civilized Europe right across their path, and are precipitating themselves, in a fury of fanaticism and greed, upon the powerless states of the interior of Africa. The European subjects of the sultan are cowed, and without foreign assistance will not risk a repetition of Batouk. The army for internal purposes is far stronger than ever, the men being the old Ottoman soldiers, brave as Englishmen, abstemious as Spaniards, to whom the Germans have lent their discipline and their drill. No force within the empire outside Arabia could resist the reorganized troops or hope to reach, as no doubt the first Mahdi if left alone might have reached, Constantinople itself. The financial difficulties of the treasury are great, but the sultans have recently risked and have survived complete repudiation, and the revenue is enough, and will remain enough, to keep the army together and supply the luxury of the palace. — MEREDITH TOWNSEND in "Asia and Europe."

III. HISTORY AND GOVERNMENT

WE cannot trace here the story of the rise and spread of Islam from its cradle in Arabia to the period of its greatest virility in 1529, when all Europe trembled at its onward sweep and conquest. We can speak only of the rise of the Ottoman empire that has been perpetuated in unbroken succession to the present time.

Near the middle of the thirteenth century a tribe of Turks, not Suljuks, left their camping-grounds in Khorassan, urged on by the Mongol invaders, and wandered into Armenia. This tribe was divided into four sections; one of these, led by Ertogrul, went into Asia Minor, and there became allied with Aladdin the Suljukian, sultan of Iconium. He settled upon the borders of Phrygia and Bithynia and there his son Othman, or Osman, who became the founder of a dynasty and an empire, was born and nurtured. The name "Ottoman Empire" or "Osmanli Turks" came from him. The name "Othman" signifies "bone-breaker."

The young man succeeded his father as the head of the tribe. He united in his character the traits of shepherd, freebooter, and warrior. Osman's ambition was fired by a dream of conquest that seated him upon the Byzantine throne. He was upon the border of the decaying Greek empire to the west, and back of him were the vast, restless populations ready to enlist under any leader of strength and action. He invaded Nicomedia July 27, 1299, from which time his reign is usually dated. This was parallel with Edward I of England, Philip the Fair of France, and

Andronicus Palæologus the elder of Constantinople. Slow encroachment was made upon the imperial domains of the Greek empire, while at the same time his authority was extended over considerable districts in the north and west of Asia Minor, including large parts of Phrygia, Galatia, and Bithynia. Prusa (Brusa) was captured and became the residence of Othman, and was the seat of his government when he died in 1326.

Othman was succeeded by Orchan, his son, who extended the boundaries of the infant state with marked rapidity. He took Nicæa, the rest of Bithynia, the greater part of Mysia, and was the first Turkish ruler to pass over into Europe. He coined money in his own name, and assumed the prerogatives of royalty, and began the systematic organization of his government. A permanent military force was established. One of his strongest military organizations was composed of the children of conquered Christians who were reared in Islam, inured from their youth to the profession of arms. These became the famous Janissaries perpetuated in the conquests of the Turkish government until the middle of the nineteenth century. They were distinguished for their valor and fanaticism. Through more than three centuries, marked by a long series of great battles, they experienced only four signal reverses. One of these was by Tamerlane, in 1402, and another by the Hungarian general, John Huniades, in 1442. The present methods of administration of the Ottoman empire are due in no small measure to the despotic nature and fanatical character of the Janissaries. Their assumption finally reached such a state that it became necessary to extirpate them by the sword to prevent their exercise of authority over the sultans themselves. This was accomplished by Mohammed II in 1826.

HISTORY AND GOVERNMENT

Amurath I succeeded Orchan in 1359. He began at once to make advance against the Greek throne, which was much weakened by its schismatic separation from the Roman church. In 1361 he took Adrianople in Europe and made it his official residence, and the first European capital of the Ottoman power. His successor, Bajazet I, changed the title of " Emir " for that of " Sultan," which name has been perpetuated. He set the example, followed so repeatedly since, of putting his only brother to death in order that he might not aspire to the throne. He extended his domains east to the Euphrates and north to the Danube. He boasted that he would yet feed his horses on the altar of St. Peter's in Rome. He was captured by Tamerlane in 1402, dying the following year in captivity. Tamerlane held undisputed sway over Asia for a few years. A son of Bajazet, Mahomet I, restored the empire of his fathers in its integrity. It was during his reign, 1413–21, that the first Turkish ambassador appeared abroad. He was sent to Venice. The sultan himself paid a visit to the emperor Manuel at Constantinople.

Without dwelling upon the successive sultans and the advances made by each, it is sufficient to record that most important of all the victories, the capture of Constantinople, the capital of the Greek empire, by Mohammed II, the seventh in succession from Othman, on May 29, 1453, in the second year of his reign. This terminated the Greek empire, 1123 years after Constantine the Great had removed his imperial throne to Byzantium, changing its name to Constantinople. Consternation prevailed among the European nations, especially in those immediately contiguous to the Mohammedan empire.

From that time to the present day, Constantinople has been the residence of the sultans ruling over the Ottoman empire, and the seat of the Turkish power. Much of the machinery of government now in use was organized and put into operation by Mohammed II. The administrative departments were constituted in what was then called " The Porte," while the head of the department was given the well-known name of " Sublime Porte." This name came from the metaphorical resemblance between a state and a house or tent. The most important part of the tent was the entrance in which the chiefs sat for the administration of justice, as well as for the performance of other duties.

Mohammed died in 1481. Succeeding sultans for a century seriously threatened the institutions of Western nations. In the religious conflicts of the sixteenth century the pope of Rome was undecided which to fear the more, the Protestants or the Turks.

The Ottoman empire reached the zenith of its power under Suliman, the tenth sultan, whose reign was the longest in the annals of the empire, from 1520–1566. He is often known in Europe as Suliman " the great " or " the magnificent," but Moslem writers name him " the lawgiver." In 1525 the French ambassador appeared at the Ottoman court. The first European states to stipulate regular capitulations with the Porte were Genoa and Venice, which accomplished this in 1453 and 1454 respectively. These were confirmed and enlarged by succeeding sovereigns to 1733. France next secured capitulations in 1528, which were afterwards amplified, renewed, and confirmed down to 1861. The first treaty relations of England with Turkey were in 1579. Other European nations followed in orderly succession, until the United States concluded its first treaty at Constantinople, May 7, 1830, which was ratified at Washington, Feb. 4, 1832.

At the beginning of the seventeenth century the Otto-

HISTORY AND GOVERNMENT

man empire covered Europe, Macedonia, Adrianople, Greece, and the greater part of Hungary, while in Asia it held all of Asia Minor, Armenia, Georgia, Daghestan, the western part of Koordistan, Mesopotamia, Syria, Cyprus, and the chief part of Arabia. In Africa, Egypt, Tripoli, Tunis, and Algiers acknowledged allegiance to the sultan at Constantinople; and the khanate of Crimea, the principalities of Wallachia, Moldavia, and Transylvania with the republic of Ragusa were vassal states. Diplomatic and commercial relations had been established between the Porte and the leading European nations. From that time the great power then possessed began to wane.

Fundamentally the laws of Turkey are based upon the teachings of the Koran. The only restraint upon the acts of the sultan are the accepted truths of Islam as laid down in the sacred book of the prophet Mohammed. Next to the Koran the authority is a code of laws formed of the supposed sayings and opinions of Mohammed, and of sentences and decisions of his immediate successors. These are called the "Multeka," and are binding upon both the sovereign and his subjects. Beyond these the will of the man who occupies the throne of the Ottoman empire is absolute and must be unquestioned by every subject.

The sultan, therefore, is at the head of every department of government, amenable to no laws except the law of the Koran. He appoints two high dignitaries, — the grand vizier, to be the nominal head of the temporal government, and the Sheik-ul-Islam, to be the head of the spiritual government. The Sheik-ul-Islam presides over the "Ulema," a body made up of the Mohammedan clergy, the great judges, theologians, and jurists, as well as the noted teachers of Mohammedan literature and science.

There is no constitution to exercise directing influence over either the sultan or his subordinates. The grand vizier is nominally at the head of the government and represents the sultan. At the present time he has come to be only the agent of the sultan in carrying out his wishes, having little authority to act independently. The privy council, over which the grand vizier presides, is composed of the following officials or cabinet officers:

>Sheik-ul-Islam
>Minister of Justice
>   "   " War
>   "   " Marines
>President of the Council of State
>Minister of Foreign Affairs
>   "   " the Interior
>   "   " Finance
>   "   " Pious Foundations
>   "   " Public Instruction
>   "   " Commerce and Public Works

The whole of the country is divided into vilayets or states, and these are subdivided into sanjaks or provinces, which, in turn, are also divided and subdivided. The ruler in a vilayet is a vali or governor-general, who receives his appointment directly from the sultan, and who, with the assistance of a provincial council, is master of the vilayet. He has power over the inferior officers of his district, whom, theoretically at least, he appoints and removes at will. There are eight of these vilayets in Europe, eleven in Asia, five in Armenia, three in Mesopotamia, six in Syria, two in Arabia, and two in Africa, making thirty-seven in all. The man at the head of each one of these states, averaging a population of about 700,000 souls each, is accountable to the sultan alone for his position and to him he makes constant secret reports. These valis are frequently recalled and more frequently changed from place to place by orders issued directly from the throne. In this way the sultan controls all parts of his dominions and personally determines the character of the administration. All policies carried out in any part of the empire are his own and cannot be otherwise under present conditions.

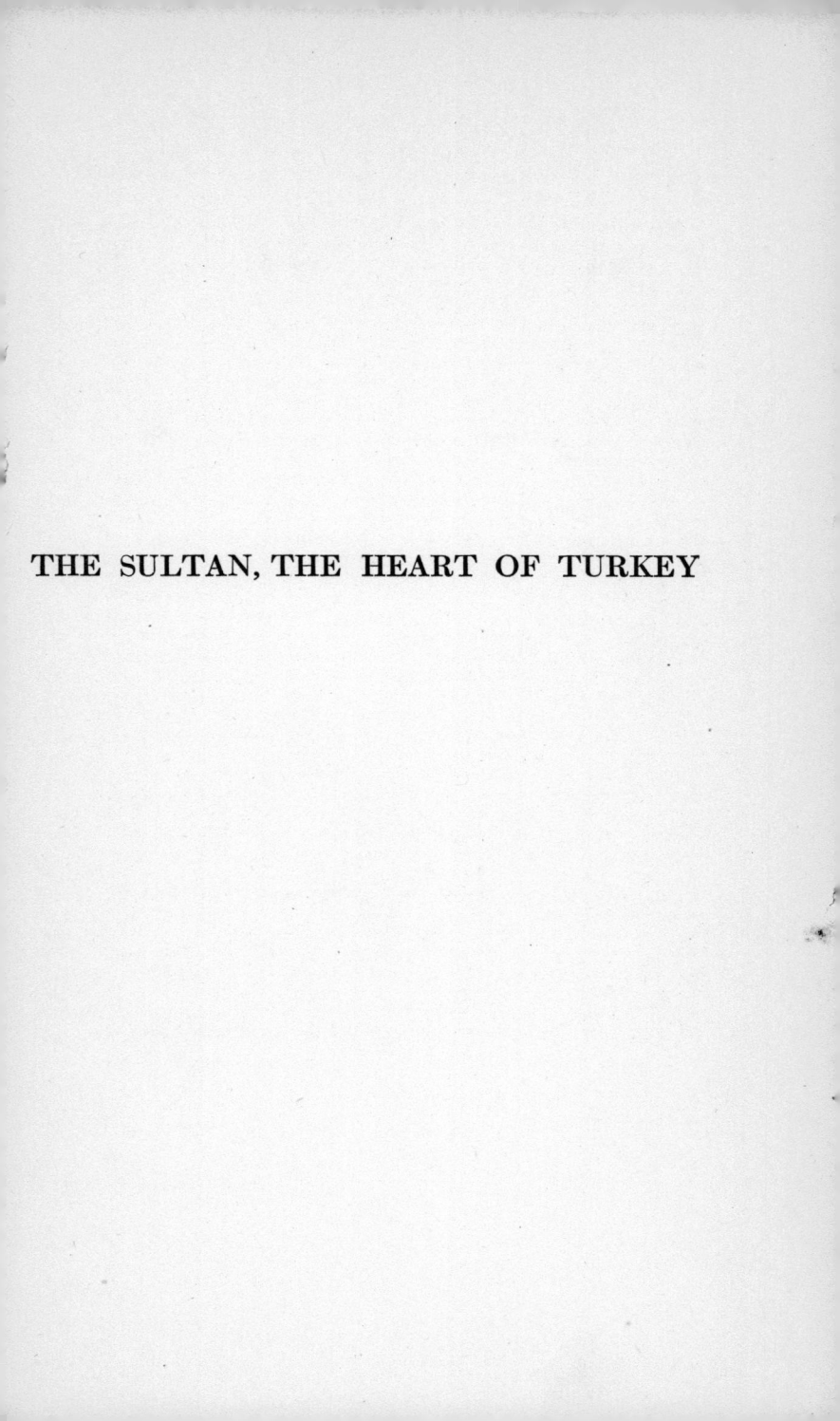

THE SULTAN, THE HEART OF TURKEY

THE general tendency of Islam is to stimulate intolerance and to engender hatred and contempt not only for polytheists, but also, although in a modified form, for all monotheists who will not repeat the formula which acknowledges that Mohammed was indeed the Prophet of God. Neither can this be any matter for surprise. The faith of Islam admits of no compromise. The Moslem is the antithesis of the pantheistic Hindoo. His faith is essentially exclusive. Its founder launched fiery anathemas against all who would not accept the divinity of his inspiration, and his words fell on fertile ground, for a large number of those who have embraced Islam are semi-savages, and often warlike savages, whose minds are too untrained to receive the idea that an honest difference of opinion is no cause for bitter hatred. More than this, the Moslem has for centuries past been taught that the barbarous principles of the *lex talionis* are sanctioned, and even enjoined by his religion. He is told to revenge himself on his enemies, to strike them that strike him, to claim an eye for an eye, and a tooth for a tooth. Islamism, therefore, unlike Christianity, tends to engender the idea that revenge and hatred, rather than love and charity, should form the basis of the relations between man and man; and it inculcates a special degree of hatred against those who do not accept the Moslem faith. "When ye encounter the unbelievers," says the Koran, "strike off their heads until ye have made a great slaughter among them, and bind them in bonds . . . O true believers, if ye assist God, by fighting for his religion, he will assist you against your enemies; and will set your feet fast; but as for the infidels, let them perish; and their works God shall render vain. . . . Verily, God will introduce those who believe and do good works into gardens beneath which rivers flow, but the unbelievers indulge themselves in pleasures, and eat as beasts eat; and their abode shall be hell fire." It is true that when Mohammed denounced unbelievers he was alluding more especially to the pagans who during his lifetime inhabited the Arabian Peninsula, but later commentators and interpreters of the Koran applied his denunciations to Christians and Jews, and it is in this sense that they are now understood by a large number of Mohammedans. Does not the word "Ghazi," which is the highest title attainable by an officer of the sultan's army, signify "one who fights in the cause of Islam; a hero; a warrior; one who slays an infidel"? Does not every Mollah, when he recites the Khutbeh at the Mosque, invoke Divine wrath on the heads of unbelievers in terms which are sufficiently pronounced at all times, and in which the diapason of invective swells still more loudly when any adventitious circumstances may have tended to fan the flame of fanaticism? Should not every non-Moslem land be considered in strict parlance a Dar-el-Harb, a land of warfare? When principles such as these have been dinned for centuries past into the ears of Moslems, it can be no matter for surprise that a spirit of intolerance has been generated. — LORD CROMER in "Modern Egypt."

IV. THE SULTAN, THE HEART OF TURKEY

THE present sultan, Abdul Hamid II, is the thirty-fourth in direct male succession from Othman and the second son of Sultan Abdul Medjid. He succeeded to the throne upon the deposition of his brother, Murad V, August 31, 1876, at the age of thirty-four. By the Turkish law of succession the crown is inherited according to seniority by the male descendants of Othman springing from the imperial harem. All children born in the harem, whether from free women or slaves, are legitimate and possess equal rights. The sultan is succeeded by his eldest son, in case there are no uncles or cousins of greater age. The present heir apparent to the throne is the oldest brother of the sultan, who outranks all of the five sons of Abdul Hamid as heir to the throne. It is not the custom of the sultans to contract regular marriages. The harem is kept full of women by purchase, capture, or voluntary offering. Most of the inmates come from districts beyond the limits of the empire, largely from Circassia.

The sultan is, without question, the most phenomenal person sitting upon any throne to-day. Educated within his own palace, having passed but once beyond the borders of the land in which he was born, he is able to outwit and outmatch in diplomacy the combined rulers of Europe. He has administered his widely-extended and varied empire in accordance with the unmodified Moslem principles of the Middle Ages, and has successfully defied all attempts upon the part of Christian nations to change his policy. Without a navy he has succeeded in averting repeated threats of attack by the strongest navies of the world. With depleted and diminishing resources he has held his creditors at bay, capitalized his indebtedness, and continued to live in lavish luxury. It is true that his refusal to comply with the demands for reform have at times in the past led to the loss of some of his possessions, still he does not seem to have learned therefrom any permanent lesson.

Turkey as a whole has never been so unrighteously governed as it is to-day, and, in spite of the pressure of European governments, there is little prospect of radical reforms so long as the present sultan sits upon the throne. While he is an astute and unprincipled diplomat and a tireless sovereign, he is not a reformer in any sense of the word. So long as he is sultan, he proposes to be master, preferring to lose entire provinces rather than to share the administration with any. He yields only when subterfuge fails and the policy of delay is rejected; after he has yielded, he devotes himself to vitiating the advantages his subjects might gain by his concessions.

Personally timid and fearful, he astonishes the world by the boldness of his strokes at home and his stubborn resistance to pressure from abroad. Himself profoundly religious, he horrifies all by the wholesale murder of his subjects through his lieutenants acting upon direct orders from the palace. This he has done repeatedly, and it is a part of his method of administering his home affairs and keeping his subjects properly subdued.

The present political, social, economic, and religious problems of Turkey center in the sultan. Few countries in the world would respond so quickly to the influence of

A GROUP OF OFFICIAL TURKS IN PRAYER FOR THE SULTAN UPON HIS BIRTHDAY

THE SULTAN, THE HEART OF TURKEY

good government, and few people would so appreciatively welcome a firm and righteous administration as the people of Turkey.

The sultan exercises his power through his army and his appointees to office. The Turks make perhaps the best soldiers in the world. They are strong, inured to hardship, uncomplaining, and practical. To them all war with non-Moslems and rebels — and they fight with no others — is holy war. Only Mohammedans are enrolled in the army, and all such, over twenty years of age in the country, are liable to military service until they are forty. The empire is divided into seven army administrative districts, in each of which is located an army corps. These are Constantinople, Adrianople, Monastir, Erzerum, Damascus, Bagdad, and the Yemen, with the independent divisions of the Hejaz and Tripoli. The infantry are armed with Mauser rifles. The effective war strength of the Turkish army is 987,900 men. The navy possesses no fighting power.

The governing force of the empire is strictly Mohammedan. The army is indeed a church militant with no unbeliever among its officers or men, except as European military experts are employed to drill and discipline the troops. The entire administration of both civil and military affairs is a religious administration. Men of other religions are asked to take part in civil affairs only when Mohammedans cannot be found to do the work required. Many high positions, even in the cabinet, have been creditably filled by Armenians and Greeks, but this is the exception and not the rule. Turkey agreed some time ago to admit Christians to her army, but has never seen her way clear to carry out the agreement. At the center of this Mohammedan administration sits the sultan, Hamid II, with his valis or governors at the head of affairs in every province, in close and constant communication with himself and carrying out his imperial will. These local governors are sustained by the Moslem army, commanded by officers who also receive their instructions directly from the palace on the Bosporus.

This is the system of administration that has become established in the Ottoman empire, and that must be borne in mind as we proceed with the study of the country, the people, their economic, social, and religious conditions.

The position of Turkey and of the Ottoman empire is unique among the countries of the world. For centuries it has stood before the world as the one great Mohammedan temporal power, with its laws and usages built upon the tenets, traditions, and fanaticisms of Islam. Every civilized definition of a government fails when applied to Turkey, and every conception of the duty of a government to its subjects is violated in the existing relations between the Turkish government and the people of that empire. Under these conditions, much worse now than they were two generations ago, mission work is carried on.

While there are many Turkish officials who keenly deplore the evils of the system, and would change if they could the untoward relations of the government to its oppressed subjects, they are powerless to act and must even conceal their dissatisfaction for fear of being branded, as many have been, as traitors to the existing rule, for which charge the penalty is banishment or death. There is a general feeling that no reform can be inaugurated or carried out so long as the present monarch sits upon the throne.

A distinguished Orientalist, intimately acquainted with affairs at Constantinople, has recently written upon the

THE SULTAN, THE HEART OF TURKEY

sultan and his diplomatic methods in the following terms. For obvious reasons the identity of the writer is concealed:

Rarely has a young sovereign been in a more desperate and apparently hopeless position than Abd-ul-Hamid occupied in the third year of his reign, 1878. His armies had been utterly beaten in a great war. His people had no confidence in their country, or their future, or their sultan. Prophecies were widely current about 1878–1882 identifying him as the last sultan of Turkey and the consummator of its ruin. The treasury was almost bankrupt. He himself had, and still has, a dislike and fear of ships, which paralyzed his fleet during the war that had just ended, and has ever since left it to rot in idleness, until there is at the present day, probably, not a Turkish ship of war that could venture to cross the Ægean Sea in the calmest day of summer.

The sultan alone in Turkey did not despair. He alone saw how the power of the sultans could be restored. And twenty-eight years after he seemed to be near the end of a disastrous and short reign he is still on the throne, absolute autocrat to a degree that hardly even the greatest of the sultans before him attained, in close communication with the remotest corners of the Mohammedan world from the east of Asia to the west of Africa, respected and powerful in Moslem lands where the name of no former sultan was known or heeded, courted by at least one leading Power in Europe and by the great American republic.

The last fact is, perhaps, the most remarkable of all in this strange history. The diplomatists of America, so strong and self-confident in their dealings with the greatest of European Powers, so accustomed to say to them all, "This is our will and intention," have for many years been the humblest and most subservient of all the Christian Powers in their attitude to Turkey, aiming always at imitating the German policy and being on the friendly side of the Turks, but forgetting that Germany has that to give which America has not, and that America has interests to protect in Turkey of a kind which Germany has not.

The sultan had the genius or the good fortune to divine almost from the beginning of his reign what only a few even yet dimly comprehend, — the power of reaction and resistance which Asia can oppose against the West. He formed the plan of consolidating the power of the entire Mohammedan world, and placing himself at the head of this power, and he has carried the plan into effect. The sultans had always claimed the position of khalif, but this had hitherto been a mere empty name, until Abd-ul-Hamid appealed from his own subjects, who rejected him, to the wider world of Mohammedans, won their confidence, and made them think of him as the true Commander of the Faithful.

One naturally asks whether this result was gained through the strength of a real religious fervor or through the clever playing of an astute and purely selfish game. While there may have been something of both elements, I do not doubt that there was a good deal of religious enthusiasm or fanaticism; the first idea could never have been struck out without the inspiration of strong religious feeling.

It used to be said about 1880 by those who were in a position to know best — no one has ever been in a position to have quite certain knowledge in Constantinople — that the sultan was a Dervish of the class called vulgarly the Howling, and that when (as was often the case) the ministers of state summoned to a council had to wait hour after hour for the sultan to appear, he was in an inner room with a circle of other Dervishes loudly invoking the name of Allah and working up the ecstatic condition in which it should be revealed whether and when he should enter the council. I do not doubt that the great idea of appealing to the world of Islam was struck out in some such moment of ecstasy. At the same time, Abd-ul-Hamid has had a good deal to gain from the success of this policy.

Europeans who have been admitted to meet the sultan in direct intercourse are almost all agreed that he possesses great personal charm and a gracious, winning courtesy. On the other hand, ministers of state used to speak with deep feeling of the insults and abuse poured on any, even the highest, who had the misfortune to express an opinion that did not agree with his wishes.

An official in the palace described very frankly — it is wonderful how freely and frankly Turks express their opinion; this seems in-

THE SULTAN, THE HEART OF TURKEY

separable from the Turkish nature — to an Englishman whom he knew well the situation in the palace at the time when an ultimatum had been presented, and before it was known what would be the issue; how the sultan was flattered up to believe that he had only to go into Egypt and resume possession, and that the English would never resist. The Englishman remarked, "But you know better than that, and of course you give better advice when the sultan asks your opinion." "God forbid," was the reply, "that I should say to the sultan anything except what he wishes me to say. No! when he asks me, I reply that of course the master of a million of soldiers has only to enter Egypt and it is his. And it is not for nothing that I do this. The sultan is pleased with me, and signs some paper that I have brought him, and it may be worth 10,000 piastres to me."

The sultan hates England with a permanent and ineradicable hatred; this feeling dominates and colors his whole policy; it is only for that reason that he tolerates Germany, which otherwise he dislikes. England has always been the friend of the Reform party in Turkey; and the sultan is the great reactionary who has trodden the Reform party in the dust. But, worse than that, England, pretending to help Turkey, took possession of Cyprus, nominally to enable her to guarantee Turkey against Russia in Asia Minor, but really (as it seems to the Turks) by pure theft, because all pretence of using Cyprus as a basis of operations against Russia in Asia Minor was abandoned in 1880, and yet England kept Cyprus.

Now to the sultan the sting lies in this, that Cyprus was his private appanage, and not part of the State. The whole revenue of Cyprus went to the sultan's privy purse. But worse still: at first the English paid over the Cypriote revenue, about £95,000 a year, to Constantinople, but after the Gladstonian government came into power, in 1880, this revenue was diverted to pay interest on the Turkish debt, emptying the sultan's private purse into the lap of the European bondholders.

The sultan, therefore, welcomed the German intervention, for the Germans encouraged him to govern as he pleased. They even persuaded him that railways were necessary for military efficiency, and showed that the Hedjaz Railway must be the foundation of his khalifate. Yet the railways that he has made, and the Moslem schools that he has founded, are the surest means of educating his people, and education is the inevitable enemy of autocracy.

The German policy has seemed to be very successful in promoting German interests in Turkey. But, after all, the ground fact is that the German policy was an opportunist policy, and the English policy, ignorant and ill-managed as it has been, was founded on deeper principles. History will record hereafter that the former proved a failure, and that the hatred of a people more than compensated for the favor of an evanescent tyrant. The same struggle is going on in Turkey as in Russia — the educated part of the people on one side, a tyranny resting on bureaucracy and obscurantism on the other. Whatever may be the faults of Abd-ul-Hamid, his worst enemy must place him on an immensely higher level than the czar on any point of view, humanitarian or patriotic, personal or political. But for England in Turkey the greatest danger is that she be tempted to Germanize her policy from experience of the apparent German success. Her policy has been, on the whole, the wiser, but it has been carried out with an ignorance of Turkish facts that is appalling.

RACE QUESTIONS AND SOME OF THE RACES

The rigidity of the Sacred Law has been at times slightly tempered by well-meaning and learned Moslems who have tortured their brains in devising sophisms to show that the legal principles and social system of the seventh century can, by some strained and intricate process of reasoning, be consistently and logically made to conform with the civilized practices of the twentieth century. But, as a rule, custom based on the religious law, coupled with exaggerated reverence for the original lawgiver, holds all those who cling to the faith of Islam with a grip of iron from which there is no escape. "During the Middle Ages," it has been truly said, "man lived enveloped in a cowl." The true Moslem of the present day is even more tightly enveloped by the sheriat.

In the third place, Islam does not, indeed, encourage, but it tolerates slavery. "Mohammed found the custom existing among the Pagan Arabs he minimised the evil." But he was powerless to abolish it altogether. His followers have forgotten the discouragement, and have very generally made the permission to possess slaves the practical guide for their conduct. This is another fatal blot in Islam.

Lastly, Islam has the reputation of being an intolerant religion, and the reputation is, from some points of view, well deserved, though the bald and sweeping accusation of intolerance requires qualification and explanation. The followers of the Prophet have, indeed, waged war against those whom they considered infidels. They are taught by their religious code that an unbelievers, who may be made prisoners of war, may rightly be enslaved. Moreover, sectarian strife has not been uncommon. Sunni has fought against Shiah. The orthodox Moslem has mercilessly repressed the follower of Abdul Wahab. Further, apostasy from Islam is punishable with death and it is not many years ago that the sentence used to be carried into effect. On the other hand, the annals of Islam are not stained by the history of an Inquisition. More than this, when he is not moved by any circumstance specially calculated to rouse his religious passions, the Moslem readi extends a half-contemptuous tolerance to the Jew and the Christian. In the villages of Upper Egypt, the Crescent and the Cross, the Mosque and the monastery, have stood peacefully side by side for many a long year. – LORD CROMER in "Modern Egypt."

V. RACE QUESTIONS AND SOME OF THE RACES

ALL questions relating to the internal government of the Ottoman empire would be greatly simplified and much more easily comprehended, were the people of Turkey substantially of one race like those of China or Japan. But this is not the case. As the Moslems overran Syria, Mesopotamia, Armenia, and Asia Minor, they conquered peoples of other races than themselves and of other religions. In their wars of conquest the Mohammedans revealed a degree of toleration which is to be commended. All conquered people were asked to embrace Islam. If they persistently refused, they were conceded the right to live upon the payment of an annual tribute *per capita*. The acceptance of this condition was an outward recognition that the Moslems were their masters, while the money thus obtained enabled the conquerors to extend their conquests. Whoever declined to accept Islam and refused to pay the life tax was put to the sword. This left within the conquered districts only two classes, the Mohammedan rulers and those who, by annual tribute, confessed themselves to be a conquered people, permitted to live from year to year by virtue of the money paid.

It is most natural that this distinction, perpetuated for thirty generations, should lead to aggravated relations of conqueror and conquered. It was inevitable that the Moslems should become imperious and the other people depressed and subservient.

DAYBREAK IN TURKEY

In order to understand certain governmental and religious phases of the Turkish empire, it is essential that we look a little in detail into the history and characteristics of these divergent elements of its population which together make up the populations of that country. It is a subject preeminently of races and religions. Within the empire there is only one unifying force and that is Mohammedanism. All who embrace Islam, irrespective of the race from which they sprang, become an integral part of the governing body. Such begin at once to use either the Turkish or the Arabic language and to bear the name "Turk."

Besides this one unifying force, there is no tendency to bring together the different races or to amalgamate them. There is little intermarriage. Each race has its own language and its distinct religion. To them all religion is racial, or, as they call it, "national." A man without a religion is beyond their conception; and under the laws of the empire he can have no place in any community or possess any rights that others are bound to respect. Each man, woman, and child must be registered upon the rolls of some national church. There his name stands, and in that record his rights inhere until he changes to Islam. Turkey allows few rights or privileges to one not a registered member of a religious community.

We will consider briefly a few of the old historical and, in some cases, once powerful races, now found in that empire, and among which mission work is carried on. Only by acquaintance with these races can we understand the real factors in the problem.

There are the many non-Moslem races of Syria, the country first overrun by the Moslem invaders as they pushed their way northward. The races who occupy that country in connection with perhaps one million Mohammedans are the Nusairiyeh, the Maronites, Greeks and Armenians, Jacobites, Druses, and Jews. The three mentioned here especially peculiar to Syria are the Nusairiyeh, the Maronites, and the Jews.

THE NUSAIRIYEH

The Nusairiyeh number a quarter of a million souls or more and are perhaps the most degraded of all of the races in Turkey. They are also most difficult to classify religiously or ethnologically. Their religion is a mixture of ancient heathenism, the survival of certain Gnostic beliefs, tinged strongly with Mohammedanism. The Mohammedans claim them, as they do the Koords and Albanians. They dwell in the mountains north of Syria and along the Mediterranean coast as far north as Cilicia. Their origin is lost in obscurity. At present they are decidedly a mixed race. Their name comes from Nusair, who led them in their separation from the Shiites, of which they were a branch. The Nusairiyeh are most reticent upon the subject of their religion. It is regarded as an unpardonable sin to reveal their religious beliefs and rites. They worship the moon, which they think is the throne of Ali, and the sun, which is the throne of Mohammed. They also worship fire, the waves of the sea, and anything that manifests power. They believe in transmigration of the soul, progress being upward or downward according to the life of the individual.

It is, in short, a rude, primitive, rough, and ignorant race, absolutely under Turkish sway and terribly oppressed. Little progress has yet been made in the line of mission work among them. The Turks guard them with a jealous eye, and the severest persecutions await all who profess Christianity, and every effort is made to prevent their education and general enlightenment.

THE MARONITES

The Syrian Maronites number not less than 250,000 and are scattered all over the Lebanon and Anti-Lebanon ranges. They are found in largest numbers in the northern districts of Lebanon and there they have control of local affairs. They are also found as far south as Mount Hermon in the country of the Druses. The hostility of these two races led to the massacres of 1860 in which thousands of the Maronites were slain. They take their name from John Maron, their first patriarch and political leader, who died in 701 A. D. They were mixed up with the Monophysite controversy in the sixth and seventh centuries. In an attempt to reconcile them, John Maron, a Monothelite (one will) leader, at the time of the Moslem invasion, conducted them into the high mountains of the Lebanon and Anti-Lebanon, where for five hundred years they maintained their independent existence in the face of every attempt to subdue or dislodge them. They developed qualities of manly strength and industry. Their language was the Syrian and their government a simple feudal system. They had a patriarch with Episcopal dioceses at Aleppo, Balbek, Jebeil, Tripoli, Ehden, Damascus, Beirut, Tyre, and Cyprus.

This interesting people was discovered to the world by the Crusaders and through them were brought under the wing of the Roman Catholic Church at the Council of Florence in 1445. They adopted the Arabic language but retained their old Syriac ritual. They are to-day recognized as followers of the Church of Rome with a form of worship somewhat modified to meet their special conditions. The Jesuits and forces of the Catholic Church have made every effort to prevent the Protestant missionaries from getting a foothold among them. Much, however, has been done for them by both the Presbyterian Board North, and the Free Church of Scotland. The Irish Presbyterian Church of Damascus is reaching the Maronites in that part of the country. Education is greatly transforming the race and through this they are becoming more and more responsive to evangelical religion.

THE DRUSES

The Druses are a smaller sect numbering probably not more than 100,000, possibly less, and occupying the Lebanon and Anti-Lebanon in touch with the Maronites. They are found as far north as Beirut and as far south as Tyre, extending even to Damascus. Their chief town is Deir-el-Kamor, about fifteen miles southeast of Beirut. They are decidedly a mixed race with the blood of the Crusaders mingling with that of native and invading peoples. They are a people of an unusually high order of intelligence and outward refinement. They are an offshoot of the Mohammedans through the fanatical, if not insane, leadership of one of the caliphs of Egypt who began to reign in 996. One Darazi who made known the claims of the caliph to divine incarnation led these people into the mountains of Lebanon and is supposed to have given them his own name.

They believe in one God and in a fixed number of human souls that can never be increased or diminished. This resemblance to the religions of India is probably due to Persian teaching. They recognize the claims upon them of no other religion, and yet with manifest indifference they join

in the prayers of the Mohammedans in their mosques and sprinkle the holy water of the Catholic Church with the Maronites, according as expediency may require. They have seven commandments:
1. Speaking the truth (only between Druses, however).
2. Combination for mutual defense.
3. Renunciation of all other creeds.
4. Social separation from all who are in error.
5. Recognition of the unity of Hakim with God.
6. Complete resignation of the will.
7. Obedience to orders.

They believe in free will and reject the fatalism of the Mohammedans.

When the Mohammedans inaugurated the massacre of the Maronites to check their growing strength under Christian enlightenment, the Druses joined with the Turks as the enemies of Christianity. It was this massacre which led to the intervention of Europe, resulting in the exclusion of Turkish officials from the Lebanon and the establishment of a special government for that district with a Roman Catholic governor and a mixed council under a constitution drawn by the European Powers. This has made a great change in the Lebanon, affording the people of that vilayet larger freedom of action and greater exemption from Turkish persecution than are enjoyed in any other part of the Turkish empire. The Druses and Maronites live on terms of harmony. They are a brave, fine-looking and enterprising people, living mostly by agriculture.

THE JEWS

The Jews are too well known in both ancient and modern history to demand space here. While they are found in

RACE QUESTIONS AND SOME OF THE RACES

considerable numbers in Syria, possibly as many as eighty thousand, they do not hold an important position in relation to the government of that country, or in the mission problems. While the Jews in Russia are always at the front, in Turkey they seldom appear. The Turks seem to have no fear that they will interfere in any way with the affairs of state.

They do not command the prominence commercially in Turkey that they do in most other countries. In the city of Constantinople it is estimated that there are seventy-five thousand Jews, and in the other large cities of the empire they exist in smaller numbers. They are an inoffensive people, attending to their own affairs and not interfering with the other races, all of whom look down upon them as inferior. In many places in the interior where they appear in small numbers they are, for the most part, extremely poor.

SYRIANS OR JACOBITES

There is probably no distinct race in Turkey that may be called Syrian. Dwelling in Syria and extending north into Mesopotamia and east towards Persia are Christian peoples who do not belong to any of the races mentioned, but who are the direct descendants of the early Christian Church. This country has been the great meeting-ground of nations, over which have swept from time to time Egyptians, Greeks, Armenians, Persians, Mongols, Koords, and Europeans of every name and race. The presence of the sacred places of the Christian faith has called forth pilgrimages and given occasion for conflicts. It was here that the early Christian Church was named, and here have dwelt some of the greatest of the fathers of the early Greek Church, such as Ignatius, Justin Martyr, and

Jerome. In those earlier days missionary influences went out from that land to other regions and countries.

Under the special effort of Constantine and his mother, Helena, pilgrims began to turn their steps towards Palestine, and monasteries sprang up all over the country. When Chosroes of Persia swept over that land, he slaughtered Christian monks by the thousand. Then came the Arabs with Mohammedanism, who converted some of the churches into mosques, but left others for the service of the Christians. Many Syrians accepted Islam and the strength of the Church waned. At the time of the crusades there were not more than five hundred thousand Christians in the country, according to some estimates. To win these the Roman pontiff had made prodigious efforts, but for the most part they refused to acknowledge the supremacy of the pope.

The Syrian Church, therefore, is the remnant which remains from the conflicts and persecutions of the last eight centuries. It does not represent a single race or people, but is able to trace its pedigree as a church back to the very beginnings of Christianity. The remnants of this early church are found throughout Palestine and northern Syria, including Damascus. They are found also in Mosul, Mardin, and northern Mesopotamia in considerable numbers. In the northern regions they are sometimes called *Jacobites*. There are many strong men among them and in some places not a little of the pride and glory of the old church remains. Some of their old churches and monasteries contain valuable manuscripts in the Syriac language of ancient date. The spoken language of these people is now, for the most part, Arabic.

They have suffered much persecution from the Mohammedans, especially from the Suljuk Turks, which had much influence in arousing the knighthood of Europe to enter upon the crusades. After the failure of the crusades these Christians were again subject to Moslem misrule at the hands of the Mohammedan sultans of Egypt and invaders from Turkey. The whole land was conquered in 1517 by the Ottoman Turk, Selim I. Except for the brief period (1832–1841) when Syria was held by Ibrahim Pasha, this country and this church have been under the rule of the sultan who sat upon the throne in Constantinople.

As the manuscript Bibles, liturgy, and church books were in Syriac, while the common people spoke and understood only the Arabic, Christianity became largely a matter of form from which the spirit had departed. The same conditions prevailed here which we shall discuss later in the Gregorian Church.

THE GREEKS

The Greeks claim that they have the oldest Christian Church, since they are the heirs to the old Byzantine empire at Constantinople, and use even now in their worship the Greek of the apostles and the liturgy of the early fathers. They constituted the majority at the first seven ecumenical councils, dominating in no small degree by their philosophy and thought the doctrines there established. They contend with the Syrian Church over priority of origin. The political history of the Greek Church began with the conversion of Constantine in 312 A. D., when persecution ceased and Christianity became the state religion.

We do not need for our present purpose to trace the history of the Church of Constantinople down to its separation from the Church of Rome in 1054, and the capture of the city by the Turks in 1453.

During this period the Church conducted a vigorous missionary propaganda. Cyril and Methodius went into Thessalonica and Bulgaria and there did substantial fundamental Christian work. Russia was also reached from this center and the czar was baptized and the nation became Christian.

In government, the Greek Church is Episcopal. The temporal power centers in the patriarch. There are several of these, the chief of whom resides at Constantinople, although the patriarchs at Antioch, Alexandria, and Jerusalem have nominally the same authority. Under Turkish rule the office of the patriarch has been exalted into practically the head of the Church, the bishops exercising spiritual authority alone. This arrangement is the same that exists in the Gregorian Church, as we shall see later. The general synod, made up of the bishops of the surrounding provinces, is presided over by the patriarchs, whom they are supposed to elect, but whose election must always be confirmed by the sultan of Turkey. The authority by which the patriarch acts comes from a firman or charter granted by the sultan.

In 1833 the branch of the Greek Church now included in the kingdom of Greece severed itself from primary dependence upon the patriarch at Constantinople. The Church of Russia, up to the middle of the seventeenth century, was holden to the Constantinople patriarch to confirm the primate of Moscow. Peter the Great in 1712 curtailed the authority of this primate, putting in his place the Holy Synod, over which the czar is supreme. These changes left the patriarch at Constantinople with authority over only the Greek churches within the bounds of the Turkish empire. The Greek Church of Roumania and Servia soon became independent and in 1870 the

RACE QUESTIONS AND SOME OF THE RACES

Church of Bulgaria withdrew and reunited under one chief bishop called the Bulgarian exarch.

One prominent fact that must be constantly kept in mind is that after these churches had separated from the mother Church and become independent of her control, they constituted what is virtually another Church. Relations one with the other were completely severed, and often violent hostility prevailed. In 1905 a severe and bloody conflict was waged in Macedonia between officers of the Greek Church who claimed allegiance to the Synod at Athens, and officers of the same Church who recognized as their head the Bulgarian exarch. Hostility was as severe and bloody as between Moslems and Christians. Church buildings were captured, the one from the other, and loyal subjects fought to the death in resistance of these attacks. This is a fact that must be taken into consideration as the various Churches and Christian sects in that part of the world are studied and their relation to Mohammedanism and the Turkish empire weighed.

We are not especially concerned here with the peculiar beliefs of this Church. We are not dealing with the question from a theological standpoint, but from the general standpoint of its relations to the government of Turkey and to the other coreligionists within the empire.

The most of the adherents of the Greek Church within the Turkish empire are Greeks. They are a strong, hardy, vigorous and intelligent race. Many of them are direct descendants, without doubt, of mighty men of valor who held their own in the face of overpowering odds in the early days of Greek chivalry. In Constantinople, where some 175,000 live to-day, they stand first among the bankers and leading merchants. Greeks figure largely in Smyrna and in fact in all of the cities of western Asia Minor, while they are found as far in the interior as Marsovan, Cæsarea and Sivas. As one goes still farther east, Greeks for the most part disappear and their place in trade and commerce is taken by Armenians. It is an interesting fact that along the upper Tigris and Euphrates rivers, where mines exist, in many instances there is a colony of Greeks close by. Tradition reports that these are descendants of the men left behind in the famous retreat of the Ten Thousand across that country to Trebizond upon the Black Sea.

These Greeks, while citizens of Turkey, it may be, for fifty generations, not infrequently refer to the king of Greece as "our king George." Along the borders of Macedonia towards Greece they cause the sultan much trouble by their sympathy with that kingdom rather than with him. For the most part, throughout Turkey they are quiet and give little trouble by revolutionary propagandism.

In educational institutions the Greek youth show superior intellectual ability and unusual eagerness. In commercial affairs they rank second to no other race and as merchants they have already gone into all the earth. Destitute of the intense national feeling of the Armenians, they have not given the Turkish government the trouble and anxiety that the Armenians have caused. As their fatherland is outside the borders of the present Turkish empire there is no fear upon the part of the Turkish rulers that they will attempt to set up an independent government. They have not, therefore, suffered the persecution that has been laid upon the Armenians.

THE ARMENIANS

WHEN I was in Constantinople I felt the restless tossings of long enthralled nationalities awaking to the new destinies that might be theirs — Armenians thirsting for their lost country and dispersed people; Bulgarians panting and striving for freedom in a Greater Bulgaria; Egyptians claiming independence; Jews praying for a return to the land of David and Solomon; Greeks dreaming strange dreams of a greater and united Greece, yes, even of an eastern empire restored to them, with Constantinople as its centre. I saw the Turk, still defiant but apprehensive, dimly conscious that the end is near at hand, lamenting the sins of his people — such sins as that the women do not wholly veil their faces, that the men do not slay the infidels. I discerned the subtle plotting of diplomacy to guard or gain the Queen City, and so the empire of the East. Everything seemed then, as now, uncertain. It might be peace, it might be war; but all were sure that the old was breaking up, whether to make way for inrushing floods of destruction, or for better days and nobler nations, none could tell. Then I went to the most sacred and vital spot of Stamboul, not to St. Sophia, which, with all the lights and prayers of Ramazan, testified only to the degradation and defeat of the purer by a coarser faith, which had become God's scourge. I went to the Bible House, and there first, while all was shaking about, I felt that I stood upon a rock, the very Rock of Ages. The old city had fallen because it was built upon a shut Bible; this city was about to fall because it was built upon the Koran. But here on the open Bible was being reared a city which hath a foundation whose builder and maker is God. — EDWARD A. LAWRENCE in "Modern Missions in the East."

VI. THE ARMENIANS

OF all the races and sects of the Ottoman empire, none except the Turks are so closely identified with the country, its progress and present conditions, as the Armenians. They have been preeminently the means and occasion for prosecuting missionary work there, and the Armenian question has been discussed in the parliaments of all Europe and even now is far from solution.

The Armenians constitute one of the two distinct Christian peoples in the empire, the other being the Greeks. They stand with the Greeks, a keen rival for the honors of antiquity, while from the Christian standpoint they hold a position entirely unique. Their antiquity, racial strength, intellectual alertness, large numbers, and importance in that empire all demand a more extended consideration.

There are two distinct sources from which account of them comes, — one, their own historians, and the other, contemporary historians. According to the former, they are the direct descendants from Noah through Japheth, who was the father of Gomer, the father of Togarmah, who begat Haig, the father of the Armenian race. It is a fact to be noted here that they always refer to themselves not as Armenians but as Haiks, and to their country as Haiasdan. They find no little difficulty in pronouncing the word "Armenia." The name "Armenians" was applied to the race by outside nations because of the exploits of one Aram, the king of Haiasdan, the seventh removed from Haik, who made many conquests and impressed the power of his arms upon the weaker people about him. To these people the Haiks were the followers of Aram and so were called Armenians. The Armenians claim that their present language, except for the changes that have crept in through the centuries, was spoken in the ark. Their traditions blend in the third and fourth centuries before Christ with many facts of Assyrian, Median, and Greek history, so it is impossible to differentiate precisely where legend ends and history begins.

There is no doubt that during the Assyrian and Median period there was in Armenia, which included the mountains of Ararat, and the upper Araxes, Euphrates and Tigris rivers, centering perhaps in the region of Lake Van, a well-organized and powerful monarchy. The ancient Assyrian records show that this people had to be reckoned with in all plans for campaigns in the Ararat country, and not infrequently the invaders were compelled to retire in apparent haste. Well-preserved inscriptions are found upon the cliffs at Van and in the same language across the country six hundred miles or more to the east, which show the presence there (700 B. C.) of a powerful and warlike people. Whether these were the progenitors of the present Armenian race or whether they were conquered by some stronger invading force, which completely dominated the country, is not as yet clear.

The last of the Haig dynasty, Vahe, formed an alliance with Darius III against the Macedonians. He was defeated by the forces under Alexander and was slain. The people were without a leader for one hundred and thirty years, and were trampled upon and plundered by invading armies from every side. About 190 B. C. two Armenian nobles arose who divided the kingdom and ruled over it. This divided kingdom was again united under Tigranes (Dickran II) in 89 B. C. In 67 B. C. the Armenians became an ally of Rome, and in 30 B. C. were made tributary.

THE ARMENIANS

For two and a half centuries thereafter the entire country was again in turmoil and political disorder. From that time to the present the Armenians have never represented a political power that needed to be reckoned with. Their people were scattered with no uniting force, without a commanding leader or a distinctive country.

A little Armenian kingdom in Cilicia in the Taurus Mountains maintained an existence until 1375 A. D. Since that time Armenians have had no political existence whatever. They have been, and are still, a people without a country, a nation without a government.

As soon as the Mohammedan invasion took place they had no alternative but to yield to their conquerors or die. It was but natural that they should scatter from the old ancestral haunts to all points of the compass, in search of more liberty and a better opportunity to secure a living. They have gone into every city, if not into nearly every village of size in the empire. Before the massacre of 1895–96 there were nearly a quarter of a million Armenians in Constantinople alone. Their energy and enterprise and industry give them prominence in trade, in the professions, and in the cultivation of the soil. They have gone far beyond the borders of Turkey, and are found to-day in nearly every country in the world. Many hold high and honorable positions in foreign lands.

Armenians exist in larger numbers still in their old haunts about Lake Van, where they constitute perhaps a majority of the population. In all the cities of Eastern Turkey, extending from the Black Sea south into northern Mesopotamia, westward to the Euphrates river, and beyond, they hold a prominent place, although they are upon the whole a minority. The rest of the population are mostly Turks, the ruling body, and the Koords. These races, especially the Turks and Armenians, live in the same towns, but never intermarry. The Koords live more by themselves in the mountains. As we pass on into Asia Minor, the Armenians decrease while the Greeks increase in numbers and in the importance of the positions they command.

The Armenians are also numerous in northern Syria, especially in the region near their last Cilician kingdom. Adana, Tarsus, Marash, Aintab, Hadjin, Oorfa and many other cities in that region have a large Armenian population. Their language is Turanian, constructed upon the Greek model, and is especially rich in its power of expressing Christian truths and sentiments. The most of the Armenians speak this tongue, but some in the mountains of Koordistan speak only Koordish, while the Armenians in northern Syria use the Turkish language. Turkish is spoken by nearly all Armenians, as well as by all the races north of Syria.

Religiously, the history of the Armenians is full of interest. Their histories claim that at the time of Christ their king Abgar, called by Tacitus the king of the Arabs, resided at Urfa in northern Mesopotamia. He is reported to have had some communication with Christ, who, at his death, through the apostle Thomas, sent Thaddeus to preach to the Armenians. The king and his court were baptized. His successor apostatized from the faith, and so Christianity was lost to the race until the fourth century. At the beginning of this century St. Gregory the Illuminator preached at the court of Armenia with such effect that from that period to this Christianity has been the national religion. The Church has held the race together. It is known as the Gregorian Church, after St. Gregory, while the people themselves always refer to their

AN ARMENIAN ECCLESIASTIC

A KOORDISH CHIEF OF SOUTHERN KOORDISTAN

church as Loosavorchagan, derived from Loosavorich, meaning "The Illuminator." As this is the national Church, all Armenian children are baptized in infancy and become members.

At first the Gregorian Church took part in the ecumenical conferences, but for some reason they had no representatives in the council which met at Chalcedon in 451 A. D. In a synod of Armenian bishops in 491 the decisions of the council of Chalcedon were rejected, and at a later synod they declared openly for the Monophysite doctrine. This led to their complete separation from the Greek Church.

Their church government is Episcopal, with the same form of patriarchal control which dominates the Greek Church in Turkey. The bishop of the main body of the Armenians resides at Etchmiadzin, their holy city, now in Russia, not far from the Turkish borders. There is also a bishop on the island of Octamar in the lake of Van, and another at Cis in Cilicia, each with a small following. The bishops have authority over the spiritual affairs of the Church, like the ordaining of priests and vartabeds, while the two patriarchs, one at Jerusalem and one at Constantinople, control its temporal affairs. As these patriarchs, and especially the one at Constantinople, are in a measure the appointees of the sultan, and as he represents his people in all their government matters, the office is largely political and secular. The importance as well as the delicacy of the position is greatly increased during the times of political unrest.

At its beginning, the Church was as pure in doctrine and practise as was the Greek Church at Constantinople. It was an important branch of the Church of Christ on earth. The location of the unprotected Armenians, in a country swept by invasion and persecutors of every kind, made the position of the Church a most trying one. As illiteracy increased, the spoken language of the people underwent marked changes. The Church possessed most sacredly guarded manuscript copies of the Scriptures and beautiful liturgies, all in the then spoken language of the people. These were read at all church services and sermons were preached by the officiating clergy. As the spoken language changed during the last ten centuries, under the blasting influence of Mohammedan rule, the sacred books of the Church ceased to speak to the people. The priests read the words of the ritual, but neither they nor the people understood it. The church was too holy a place in which to make use of the vulgar vernacular, so the sermon was discontinued because there was no one to preach in the classic tongue of the race.

Under these conditions the Christianity of the Gregorian Church became, for the most part, a religion of form, from which the spirit had departed. Thus bereft of the true power of Christianity and subject to the temptations and persecutions of the Moslems among whom they dwelt, it is not strange that the Christianity of the Gregorian Church lost its vital power.

MOSLEM PEOPLES

WHAT was said above concerning Islam as the hereditary faith of the Ottoman Turk does not hold true of the other Moslem races of Turkey. Koords, Circassians, Albanians — nearly half as many, all together, as the Turks — are, at best, but half Mohammedan. To a large extent the profession of Islam by Koords and Circassians is purely outward and formal, while their esoteric faith is a mixture of Mohammedanism, Christianity and heathenism. In grouping and generalization we cannot go farther than the statement just made. Take the Koords alone. There is almost infinite variety in their religious beliefs and superstitions. It is well known that there are whole villages among them ready to declare themselves Christians, could they be assured of protection in so doing. The Moslem Albanians — somewhat more than half the race — are more bigoted and violent Mohammedans than the Turks, just as the Janissaries, likewise of Christian origin, who were compelled from childhood to embrace Islam, out-Heroded Herod in the fanaticism of their anti-Christian zeal.

With the exception of the Albanians, Islam has, in all the centuries of the reign of the Ottoman Power over these lands, made very slight gains from the Christian races. The number of Greek, Armenian, Bulgarian, Roumanian, Servian, Bosnian, or Montenegrin Mohammedans is insignificant. Of these seven races, for hundreds of years under Moslem sway, the number to-day free from Ottoman control is nearly equal to the entire population, Moslem and Christian, now directly under Turkish domination. — From "The Mohammedan World of To-day."

VII. MOSLEM PEOPLES

THE KOORDS

BESIDES the Turks and Armenians, no race in Turkey has commanded more attention during the past two decades than the Koords. They have attracted the notice of the world by their large part in the Armenian massacres in 1895-96 as well as by their relations to the sultan himself through the organization and arming of the Hamidieh cavalry within the last quarter of a century. They were almost unknown and unheard-of except locally until they came into prominence at the time of the siege of Erzerum by the Russians in 1876, when the Koords were used by the Turks in defense. They rendered little real service, however.

Whatever else may be said, this race has now to be reckoned with in all plans for propagating Christianity in any form in Eastern Turkey and western Persia, as well as in all questions of order in that region. Sometimes they are in open conflict with the Turks, and troops are mobilized and sent against them in their mountain fastnesses. Again they are provided with arms by the government and sent out to subdue and suppress revolutionary bands of Armenians who are more ambitious than discreet in their endeavors to obtain liberty.

Little is known of the origin and history of this wild and most interesting people. They probably are the direct descendants of the Karduchi, who occupied the same plateaus and commanded the same mountain passes that the Koords now hold. It is probable that they are

DAYBREAK IN TURKEY

not a race by themselves, but a collection of tribes with little among them all that is common except their hardihood, roughness, and tendency to plunder. One chief, whom the writer knew, declared that his ancestors came to the upper waters of the Tigris from Mesopotamia some eight centuries ago, and, after conquering the region, ruled it as feudal lords. That form of government is in existence among them even at the present time. Undoubtedly the word Koord, Kurd, Gutu, Gardu, or Karu, has been promiscuously applied to any mountain race, clan, or tribe occupying the upper waters of the great rivers in that part of the empire, if they were not already claimed by another race.

There are some marked distinctions between the peoples called Koords. Some are nomadic and pastoral, taking their flocks into the north of Armenia as the summer advances, and returning to the warmer regions of the south as it recedes. These live almost entirely in black tents, and, while they steal, are not generally robbers. Others settle in villages and the men devote their time usually to robbing traders and caravans passing through their country, and levying blackmail upon the Armenians who dwell upon their borders. It is this class who cause both the Turkish government and the Armenians the most trouble. A chief, whom the writer knew personally, and at whose castle he has often passed the night, boasted that he owned nearly four hundred villages with the adjacent land, and could throw, within two days' notice, two thousand armed horsemen into a fight anywhere within the bounds of his territory. He said that he had over three hundred armed men out upon the road most of the time. His castle had dungeons, and was, to all intents and purposes, a fort.

These various Koordish leaders not only have little

MOSLEM PEOPLES

in common, but they are frequently in open conflict one with another. Could these people unite under a bold leader and form an alliance with the Arabs of the south, nothing in Turkey could stand against them. Many renowned leaders from among the Koords have appeared from time to time. Saladin, a noted ameer at the time of the crusades, was a Koord.

They occupy the mountainous regions throughout Eastern Turkey, reaching far down the Tigris to Mosul and into Mesopotamia, extending into Persia upon the east and coming west as far even as Anatolia. The mass of the Koords dwell within this area, but not a few are found outside. An estimate given of their numbers places it as high as 3,000,000.

Their languages are unclassified. There are two of them, neither of which ever was put into writing except within the last generation, so that the spoken tongues of those professing to speak the same language greatly differ in different parts of the country. Their speech is rough, like the life they live, and resembles in no small degree the barren cliffs amid which they dwell.

Some years ago Sultan Hamid II conceived the idea of subduing the Koords in the eastern part of his dominions by calling the chiefs to Constantinople and making them each commander of a body of their own people, giving this troop his own name as a special honor. The chiefs were to provide the men and the horses and the sultan furnished the equipment. The proposition was most acceptable to the Koordish nobles, for it provided them with modern equipments of warfare and at the same time stamped their acts, even of depredation, with official authority. Under the new dispensation, whoever offered resistance to a Koord armed with a government rifle, by that very act put himself into open rebellion against the government. These conditions prevail at the present time in the Erzerum, Bitlis, Diarbekr and Van vilayets along the Russian frontier. Much of the trouble of the last fifteen years in these regions is due to this fact. Were it not that the Koords are urged by the government to take aggressive measures against the resident Christian population, conditions there would be better than they are at the present time.

It is often stated that all Koords are Mohammedans. The Turks take this ground, as they do regarding the Albanians of Macedonia. The fact is that few of the Koords are good Moslems. They do not hesitate to put out of the way a Turkish tax-collector who makes himself obnoxious. The fact that he is a brother Moslem interposes no obstacle. Many of them observe few of the rites and customs of Islam, and one tribe, at least, living along the upper waters of the Euphrates openly declares that it is not Mohammedan. The writer, in conversation with a leading man of that tribe, said, "You are a Mohammedan." With great indignation he spat into the air, and, beating upon his breast, he said, "I am a Koord; Moslems are dogs." They have certain religious rites which greatly resemble some of the Christian customs, as, for instance, they have a service in which bread dipped in wine is put into the mouths of the kneeling participants by their religious leader. These people often tell the Armenian Christians that their sympathy is with them rather than with the Turks.

Owing to the claim of the Turks that all Koords are Mohammedans, missionaries have not been able to inaugurate special work among them. Throughout the country called Armenia and where the Armenians are the most numerous, there also the Koords are found in the largest numbers. Frequently they reside in the same city, side by side, but more often the Armenians dwell in the plains, where they are the cultivators of the soil, while the Koords live higher up the mountains. A study of the regeneration of the Turkish empire cannot be complete without giving large consideration to this ancient, wild and violent people.

THE TURKS

In Turkey the word " Turk " is used only to designate a Mohammedan. A Greek who had accepted Islam would at once be called a " Turk." It would be said of him that " he had Turkofied himself." In its ordinary use, therefore, in Turkey it signifies a religious belief and that alone. The same may be said of the other names for nationality, such as Armenian, Greek, Jacobite, Yezidi, Koord, etc. Instead of using the word " Mohammedan " at this point we will consider this part of our subject under the title " The Turks," thus keeping the national and religious parallel intact.

The Turks of Turkey comprise every race that has ever lived within its territory and has accepted Islam. As the people of the different races embrace Islam, they come at once into the Mohammedan body and are in a large measure unified with it by the common customs imposed upon them through the government and by their religion. These assimilated races marry and intermarry so that to-day, outside of Arabia, where the race has been kept more free from mixture, it is difficult to find among the Turks a clear racial type.

The original Turkish people were invaders, coming into the country from the north and east for plunder and conquest. As soon as these conquering hordes accepted Islam, every victory over a foe meant new women for the harem and added men who chose Islam to tribute or death. When the country had been overrun and Turkish rule was established, there was exhibited the spectacle of a Mohammedan body of officials from every race of the East, scattered over all parts of the empire, except possibly some sections of Koordistan and Arabia, administering a government over the other races dwelling among them. The Turks alone could hold office, serve in the army, collect the taxes, and control affairs. In Arabia the rulers or Turks (not so called there, however) comprised the main part of the population and so had things their own way. In all other sections of the country, other races, and not infrequently races of strength and energy who had occupied that same territory for generations before Mohammedanism arose, looked upon the Turk as an intruder and were not slow to make him aware of the fact. These were, for the most part, disorganized, and, by Turkish law, disarmed, so that little could be done to change local conditions.

The Druses of Syria, the Koords in Eastern Turkey, and the Albanians of Macedonia were reckoned as Mohammedans by their rulers. As these people had few religious convictions of any kind, and as the Mohammedan yoke placed upon them did not seem heavy, they fell in with the idea in so far as it seemed to conserve their interests to do so. Even at the present time, it is not clear how sincerely these races are Mohammedan. It is thought by many who have been among them that their Mohammedanism is largely in name. During recent years, undoubtedly influences have been brought upon the Koords which bound them more closely to the sultan, although this is not true of all classes of Koords.

Years of Turkish rule, by which the non-Moslem subject is looked down upon as a "Raya" who has no rights that a Mohammedan is bound or expected to respect, has made the Turk selfish and cruel, while it has hardened the Rayas, and made them hate the government. It has come to be generally understood that the government exists only for the Turks, to serve whom the Rayas are permitted to live. Through several centuries of Turkish rule, when the Raya subjects of the Turks were in grossest ignorance and widely scattered in the country, they came to accept in stolid silence the situation as divinely ordained. Something of the fatalism of their masters seemed to settle down upon even the Christian subjects and, with little complaint, almost human slavery was accepted.

If the immediate possessions of Turkey include a population of about 24,000,000, probably 6,000,000 of these are nominal Christians, and perhaps 1,000,000 are neither Christians nor Mohammedans.

It should be said that among the Turks are found men of great strength of intellect, and not a few of high character. Every one who has been in the country speaks of men of this class whom he has met. All would probably agree with the statement that the Turk as a whole is far better than his government.

It should also be stated that in recent years the Turks themselves have been more boldly open in expressing their intense dissatisfaction with the methods of government administration, especially in the eastern part of the country. The New Turk Party, so called, has no one knows how many followers, but undoubtedly it represents the modern spirit of unrest and progress.

OTHER RACES

We need not speak at length of the Circassians, who in some respects are the most interesting race in Asiatic Turkey. These are Mohammedans who came into Turkey in large numbers after the Russian conquest of the Caucasus. Their business is primarily robbery. They are a race which must be reckoned with in the northern half of Asia Minor. We must pass over the Turkmen, or Turkomans, who can be traced back at least eight centuries. These are also Mohammedans and nomads in their habits. They are found in considerable numbers, scattered mainly over the southern half of Asia Minor. There are also the Albanians in the western part of European Turkey, able to substantiate their claim of being one of the purest and oldest races in Europe. These number perhaps two million souls, and are more united as a race than either the Circassians or the Turkomen. All three of these peoples are nominally Mohammedans, and from them have come some of the ablest and best of the Turkish officials.

The Bulgarians have a government of their own, practically independent of Turkey. Many of these, however, dwell in Macedonia, together with Turks, Albanians, and Greeks, and so constitute an important part of the Macedonian question. These are Christian and were originally a part of the Greek Church, with headquarters at Constantinople. They are a sturdy, vigorous, and intelligent race.

Space forbids the mention of other minor races like the Yezidis, neither is there call for a description of the Arabs who dwell in Arabia and northward.

It is sufficient to say that all these divergent, crude, and often hostile races, each with a religion differing

MOSLEM PEOPLES

from that of all others, together constitute the people of the Turkish empire. The dominating class is the Turk, representing the Mohammedan faith, but far from harmonious even among themselves, except as they are practically united in a common hatred of the Christians and in a common purpose to keep them from gaining supremacy in wealth, number, intelligence, or influence.

Outside of the large coast cities there are but few people in Turkey who are not native to the country. Turkey has offered little attraction to people of other countries for colonization. Far more are seeking to leave that country than are attempting to enter it. The exactions of the government upon all who dwell within the empire, the insecurity of the protection afforded to life and property, and the risks which gather about trade and commerce are not calculated to attract foreign capital or induce natives of other lands to immigrate there.

TURKEY AND THE WEST

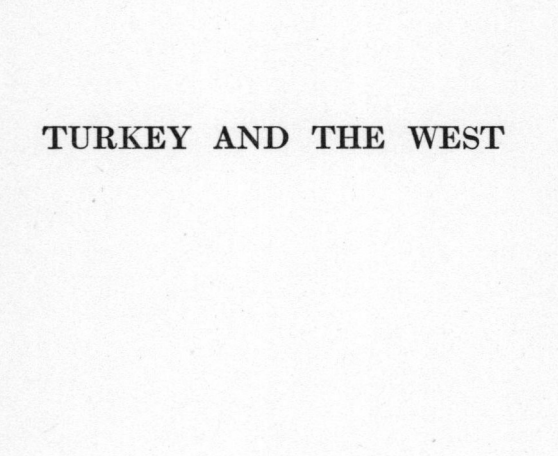

ONLY last year the Arabic paper, Es-Zahir, published in Egypt, said: "Has the time not come yet when uniting the suppressed wailings of India with our own groans and sighs in Egypt, we should say to each other, Come, let us be one, following the divine words, 'Victory belongs to the united forces'? Certainly the time has come when we, India and Egypt, should cut and tear asunder the ties of the yoke imposed on us by the English." On the other hand, Mohammed Husain, the editor of a paper at Lahore, wrote a treatise on Jihad (1893), stating: "The present treatise on the question of Jihad has been compiled for two reasons. My first object is that the Mohammedans, ignorant of the texts bearing on Jihad and the conditions of Islam, may become acquainted with them, and that they may not labor under the misapprehension that it is their religious duty to wage war against another people solely because that people is opposed to Islam. Thus they, by ascertaining the fixed conditions and texts, may be saved forever from rebellion, and may not sacrifice their lives and property fruitlessly nor unjustly shed the blood of others. My second object is that non-Mohammedans and the government under whose protection the Mohammedans live, may not suspect Mohammedans of thinking that it is lawful for us to fight against non-Mohammedans, or that it is our duty to interfere with the life and property of others, or that we are bound to convert others forcibly to Mohammedanism, or to spread Islam by means of the sword."

So the question of "religion and the sword" is still an open one among Moslems. It must needs be so long as they obey the Koran and tradition, for Mohammed said, "He who dies and has not fought for the religion of Islam, nor has even said in his heart, 'Would to God I were a champion that could die in the road of God,' is even as a hypocrite." And again, still more forcibly, "The fire of hell shall not touch the legs of him who is covered with the dust of battle in the road of God." In spite of cruelty, bloodshed, dissension and deceit, the story of the Moslem conquest with the sword of Jihad is full of heroism and inspiration. — S. M. ZWEMER, F. R. G. S. in "Islam."

VIII. TURKEY AND THE WEST

SELIM III, sultan of Turkey from 1789–1807, more formally and openly displayed the spirit and purpose of reform than had any of his predecessors. He had been carefully educated, and conceived the bold design of becoming the regenerator of the empire. He erected a printing-press at Scutari, welcomed intelligent foreigners, employed Christian workmen, and, among many other things, changed the system of taxation. He also called in European generals to train his army, and sought advice from the European residents of his capital. In the meantime, the invasion of Egypt by Napoleon had stirred up the passions of the populace of Constantinople, and the sultan with his unpopular reform measures tottered upon his throne. Russians marched into the Danubian provinces, while a British fleet passed the Dardanelles and anchored at the mouth of the Bosporus. The Janissaries mutinied in 1807 and Selim's rule ceased. These internal imbroglios had attracted the attention of the world to Constantinople and Egypt, if not to all Turkey.

After the brief reign of Mustipha IV, Mahmud II ascended the throne in 1808. He possessed extraordinary energy and force, and warmly espoused the reform measures of Selim. Resisting Russia's demand that all Greeks in Turkey should be placed under the immediate protection of Russia, he was soon at war with that country. Napoleon prevented the occupancy of Constantinople by the Russians, but most of the Danube province was lost. A Hellenic revolution was later fermented which broke into open conflict early in the beginning of mission work in Turkey.

Turkey as a government and as a factor in the relations of Russia to Europe was thus brought to the attention of the West. At the same time there was a revival of interest in the Jews, both in Europe and in the United States. There was a restudying of history and prophecy with new interpretations, which led to the formation of societies to circulate among them the New Testament and to preach to them the gospel of Christ. Naturally, Palestine and Syria came first of all to be recognized as a land that had peculiar claims upon Christians. There was a wide-spread belief that the Jews were about to return to their ancestral home, and that such return would be limited only by the obstructions put in their way by the Ottoman government. Levi Parsons, the first American missionary to Palestine, said, in 1819, just before sailing, "Destroy the Ottoman empire and nothing but a miracle will prevent the Jews' immediate return from the four winds of heaven." It was natural that, in their judgment, missionaries ought to be there to receive them when the Ottoman empire, then apparently in its death struggle, tottered to its fall.

Moreover, the Turkish empire embraced the lands of the Bible. There was in the minds and hearts of American Christians not a little of the spirit of the crusaders of the middle ages. Why should the soil trodden by the feet of the prophets and apostles, yes, even by the Lord himself, remain a stranger to the voice of the preacher of righteousness and untouched by the feet of the modern apostle? The instructions given to the first missionaries to Turkey dwelt upon this impressive and moving fact, as did the early letters of the missionaries. Unlike the crusaders, these aimed at a purely spiritual conquest, but it included the Christian subjection of all races and peoples.

As a part of this same impulse may be placed the interest in the historic Greek and Syrian Churches. Students of Church history were profoundly moved as they learned of the decadence of vital Christianity in these Churches, and they were thrilled with the desire to inaugurate among them a revival that should restore them to their former prominence and power. The purpose to reach Mohammedans does not appear prominent in the earlier documents of this period, although it is not by any means entirely wanting.

In view of these facts and also since Turkey was the most accessible to America of any Asiatic country, it is not strange that in 1819, with unusual enthusiasm, two missionaries, Levi Parsons and Pliny Fisk, were set apart for work in Turkey by the American Board of Commissioners, with special reference to the Jews in Palestine.

As a strategic center in which to begin to prosecute missionary work, few countries are more attractive than Turkey. It lies along the southern border of Russia throughout its entire length, except as separated by the Black Sea. Upon the east it borders upon Persia, and constitutes almost the only approach to this country of the shah, as well as to the Caucasus possessions of the czar. Arabia, Egypt, and North Africa all border upon the same Mediterranean Sea, and many important islands like Cyprus and Crete lie but little off its coast.

Constantinople, the capital of the Ottoman empire, occupies the most strategic position of any city in Europe and dominates both the European and Asiatic sides of the Bosporus. To this center all the great and historic cities of Turkey look for political direction, and to it come sooner or later representatives of every tribe and race in the empire. All traffic from the Black Sea to the outer world and even from Persia and southern and eastern Russia must perforce pass through Constantinople and the Dardanelles. It stands upon the highway and at the crossroads of commerce and travel. As a base for missionary operations, not only upon Turkey but upon adjacent countries as well, it is unexcelled. Smyrna upon the Grecian Sea, with immense populations behind it, by the strategic force of its location, commanded the early attention of those sent out to explore for location. Beirut in Syria attracted for the same reason the attention of the missionaries to Palestine.

There is an advantage in carrying on missionary work among sturdy races. When such are converted, they become a force in the work of the Church, the conduct of Christian institutions, and the propagation of the gospel. No country in the world could present such an array of ancient, historic, and hardy races as Turkey. Race survival there was under the law of the survival of the fittest. None but the invincible remained. Some had proven themselves invincible by arms, others had conquered by superior intelligence, strategy, and cunning. Each race remained because, in some particular, it had an advantage over its natural and persistent antagonists. The very fact that these races had kept themselves apart, resisting gradual absorption while repelling open attempts at conquest, and all for twenty centuries or more, testifies to their sturdy worth.

Some of these, like the Greeks, Armenians, Jews, and Arabs, had been masters of an ancient and proud civilization, in which learning had high place and religion was supreme. There was no ground for questioning native ability to grasp the principles of Christianity when once these peoples were enlisted. A modern Church and a modern civilization built upon such historic races, and propagated by such men, could not fail to become an irresistible force in that needy land. It is no wonder that the officers of the American Board of Missions early concluded that the Ottoman empire was a strategic point in which to plant modern Christianity and the institutions which it fosters and propagates.

While the sultan represents one sect of Mohammedanism, namely, the Sunni, and the Persians another, the Shiah, between whom there has existed great and often bloody hostility, yet the Persian Mohammedans make their pilgrimages to Mecca, pray towards that holy of holies, and reverence the sacred relics in the keeping of the sultan. However much the shah may bluster, he listens when the sultan speaks. His country can find outlet in the West only across Turkey, and much that comes from the outside world comes through some part of the Turkish empire. As the Nestorians and Armenians are found upon both sides of the line, and constitute the chief non-Moslem populations of Persia, it was most natural to connect the mission work of Persia directly with that in Turkey. Such a connection holds to the present time. In many respects Turkey was the key to Persia and is to-day.

At the beginning of mission operations, Russia was especially open to the circulation of the Scriptures in the vernacular. It was hoped and expected that soon the entire country would be accessible for direct Christian and educational operations among the millions of that empire. The whole Caucasus region can be easily approached by no other route than the Black Sea. The

Armenians dwell in large numbers in that section of the country and are constantly passing back and forth in trade and commerce. Constantinople lies at the crossing of all roads from the Black Sea regions and beyond to the outer world and the West.

The Balkan peninsula and Macedonia, lying to the north and west, also center in the capital of the Ottoman empire. As the seat of government for Macedonia and the province of Adrianople, all political influence and movement are that way. For generations it was the capital of the Balkan provinces and even yet it is the great metropolis to which merchants, students, and workmen go for a longer or a shorter period of residence abroad. There is no other center so well calculated to be the base of operations upon all that region.

The American Board was organized in 1810 and its first missionaries were sent out in 1812. These went to the farther East, to India and Ceylon. It was not the intention of the Board to confine its foreign operations to these two countries. Christian leaders in America were surveying the world for the purpose of finding other countries in which to establish Christian missions. Explorations into the western parts of our own country resulted in beginning work among the Indians as early as 1816. It is not surprising that in their survey of the wide world, its special needs and promising openings, attention should have been early called to Turkey.

A STRATEGIC MISSIONARY CENTER

IN Constantinople one does not fail to meet Greeks and Armenians who are bright and entertaining and obliging, or Mohammedans who are noble and courteous, and thoughtful enough to make their acquaintance an acquisition. But every study of the people in mass is a revelation of arrested development, absence of initiative, and general uselessness by reason of narrow selfishness. The city, and with it the millions to whom the city is model, seems hostile to what is best in the world's work. High-sounding phrases of lofty principle are heard in the city. Custom provides for this much of concession to the sensibilities of others. But the centuries seem to have frayed off the last semblance of meaning from the words. To quote a remark of a sage official in India which applies to the whole of Asia, "Whilst the mouth is proclaiming its enlightenment and progress, the body is waddling backward as fast as the nature of the ground will permit." The bane of Constantinople is not solely poverty of resources; it is poverty of ideals.— HENRY OTIS DWIGHT, LL. D. in "Constantinople and its Problems."

IX. A STRATEGIC MISSIONARY CENTER

WHILE the political and commercial importance of Constantinople is supreme, when considered in relation to the Powers of Europe and the far East, this is insignificant in comparison with its religious importance in relation to the Mohammedan world. So far as we can learn, this fact did not receive large consideration at the time missions in Turkey were begun. The truth is that it did not then hold the commanding relations to the Mohammedans of other countries that it holds to-day. The present reigning sultan, Hamid II, has done more than any of his predecessors to secure for himself recognition by all the faithful as the one supreme head, the caliph of Islam. He has sent presents with messages of sympathy and encouragement to Mohammedans in India, China, and Africa, and these have been received as from the great living head of the Moslem faith. When our government found itself in possession of a country in which a Mohammedan ruler was enthroned, it found it convenient to carry on negotiations for submission through the sultan of Constantinople. There are probably 230,000,000 Mohammedans in Turkey, Europe, Persia, Africa, India, China and other countries, who look upon the sultan of Turkey as the representative on earth of their revered prophet Mohammed. As such, he does not possess or assume temporal authority, or even well-defined spiritual prerogatives, but he does command an influence that has been secretly discussed in many European cabinets, and which has been taken into consideration in dealing with Moslem races and in administering ultimata to the head of the Ottoman empire. The sultan clearly represents a temporal and a religious power. The strength of the temporal influence lies in his relations religiously, not only to his own mediate and immediate subjects, but to all followers of the prophet Mohammed, whatever language they speak and in whatever land they dwell.

The official title of the sultan is padishah, father of all the sovereigns of the earth. This is the name exclusively used by the Turks in official communications. He is also called Imam-ul-Musselmin, the supreme pontiff of all Mussulmans or Mohammedans; Zilullah, the shadow of God; and Hunkiar, the slayer of infidels. By these and other similar titles he is known as far as the Mohammedan religion has gone. No one else claims such honors and to him they are conceded. Destroy his religious power and he would be the most impotent of monarchs, but with it he has defied for three generations the efforts of the Powers of Europe to secure some degree of justice and freedom for his oppressed subjects.

The sultan holds his religious power through two important facts. The first is that the two sacred cities of Islam in Arabia are within his empire and under his control — Mecca, the birthplace of the prophet, and Medina, which contains his tomb. This sacred territory is prohibited to infidels, but is the goal for tens of thousands of Moslem pilgrims each year. There is no faithful follower of Mohammed who does not dream of the time when he will be so blessed as to kiss the black stone of the Kaaba, drink of the well of Zemzem, or have a part in the prolonged ritual which shall entitle him during the rest of his life to the honored name of *Haji*.

THE BOSPORUS, CONSTANTINOPLE

A MOUNTAIN VILLAGE IN EASTERN TURKEY

A STRATEGIC MISSIONARY CENTER

The Mohammedans believe that the black stone came down from heaven and was connected with all the patriarchs and prophets, beginning with Adam. This is the great destination of all pilgrimages, as well as the earthly center of the Mohammedan world. To this point all faithful Moslems turn five times each day when they pray, and the lips which are permitted to kiss it are thrice blessed. Around this have grown up the Kaaba, the enclosing mosque, and other accessories too many even to name, all together constituting the holy temple of Islam where no infidel foot is permitted to tread, and upon which no vulgar Christian eye may look.

Medina, which contains a mosque supposed to cover the burial-place of Mohammed, is some seventy miles away. All faithful Moslems should visit Mecca once during their lives, but to add a visit to Medina increases their merit in the world to come. Outside of these sacred precincts all may travel, but woe be to the bold investigator who seeks to penetrate to the holy of holies of Islam. For the protection of these sacred cities the sultan of Turkey makes provision. He guards their sanctity against infidel invasion, and provides, as occasion may demand, a holy carpet for the holiest place. His soldiers safeguard the pilgrims, and his name is constantly appealed to as the slayer of infidels and shadow of God. The pilgrims from Africa, from Mindanao, from China and India and Ceylon, all return from these shrines of their faith indelibly impressed with the mighty power of him who rules at Constantinople.

The other fact which gives the sultan power over all Mohammedans is his custody of the Hall of the Holy Garment, which is next to the Kaaba, and perhaps upon a parity with it for sanctity. This hall is in the seraglio, upon the point of old Byzantium, which projects out into the Bosporus, dividing it from the Sea of Marmora. In it lie the mantle of the prophet Mohammed, his staff, his saber, his standard, and other relics. Among these, enclosed in a casket of gold, are two hairs from his beard. The sultan is supposed to make an annual visit to these sacred relics, of which he alone is keeper and guardian. The standard of Mohammed is the standard of Islam, consisting of a green silk flag about two feet square, embroidered with the inscription " There is no God but Allah and Mohammed is his prophet." It is said to have been carried by Mohammed himself and has since been regarded as the sacred standard of the entire Moslem world. If publicly borne by the sultan in the great mosques of Constantinople it would, it is said, be the signal for a general religious war. It is thought by many that should the sultan choose to use the power he possesses in this standard he could with it summon to his assistance all true Moslems and hurl them in fanatical zeal and fury against any infidel force. It is known everywhere that this standard and these relics are in the possession of the ruler of the Ottoman empire, and thus the sultan stands almost in the place of the prophet himself.

When Moslems pray they pray towards Arabia under the rule of the sultan, and when they think of their holy prophet their minds turn to the relics at Constantinople. In the face of these facts, it requires no demonstration to show that Constantinople and the Turkish empire constitute the political and religious center of Islam. Other countries may be important, this is supreme. Mecca and Medina cannot yet be entered, but Constantinople and all the rest of the Turkish empire is, by treaty, accessible

A STRATEGIC MISSIONARY CENTER

for residence to the Christian of every race and name. To begin mission work here was to start at the fountainhead.

The fact that Christian preachers and teachers are permitted to reside at Constantinople and freely preach their faith, cannot but have favorable influence over intolerant Moslems in remote parts. They all have faith in the power of the sultan as well as in his supreme wisdom. If *he* permits this, why should *they* object? In several instances in India, when the writer was conversing with Mohammedans, it was almost amusing to see the keen interest they manifested in the progress of Christianity in Turkey. They were ignorant but were ready to listen, and undoubtedly went away to ponder upon what they had heard. Evidently one thing that impressed them was that while the sultan of Turkey is a mighty ruler he does not prohibit the teaching of Christianity, even within the Throne City. If he does not prohibit it, perhaps it is not so bad a religion after all.

It is also of no little value to print and send out from Constantinople large quantities of Turkish literature, and from Beirut, Arabic literature, the two languages which are most widely read by the Mohammedans. Every volume thus printed bears the stamp of approval by the government of his imperial majesty the sultan, assuring all who read that the book was issued with his sanction and authority. Under these circumstances a publishing house at Constantinople is calculated, by its very location, to reach millions who might otherwise refuse to read what is printed. In Arabia an Arabic Bible, at first rejected because it is an infidel book, is later accepted because it bears upon its title page the authoritative permission of his imperial majesty. As a strategic center for Christian work, calculated directly and indirectly to reach the two hundred and thirty million who bear the name of the prophet of Arabia, there is no place that can compare with Constantinople, resting upon two continents and swaying the most mighty religious empire on earth.

SOCIAL, MORAL AND RELIGIOUS
CONDITIONS

THE second cause of the continuance of the Ottoman dominion has been less accidental. Like the early caliphs, and indeed all able Mussulman dynasties except the Persian, the ruling house of Turkey has for all these centuries maintained unbroken the principle that, apart from creed, ability is the only qualification for the highest service. Outside the navy, a Turkish grandee must be a Mussulman; but that granted, there is no obstacle of birth, or cultivation, or position standing in any man's path. Even slavery is no barrier. Over and over again, a sultan apparently at the end of his resources has stooped among the crowd, clutched a soldier, a slipper-bearer, a tobacconist, a renegade, given him his own limitless power, and asking of him nothing but success, has secured it in full measure. Equality within the faith, which is a dogma of Islam, and next to its belief in a "sultan of the sky," its grand attraction to inferior races, has in Turkey been a reality as it has been in no other empire on earth, and has provided its sovereigns — who, be it remembered, fear no rival unless he be a kinsman, an Arab, or a "prophet" — with an endless supply of the kind of ability they need. The history of the grand viziers of Turkey, were it ever written, would be the history of men who have risen by sheer force of ability — that is, by success in war or by statesmanship, or, in fewer instances, by that art of mastering an Asiatic sovereign and his seraglio in which fools do not succeed. The sultans have rarely promoted, rarely even used, men of their own house, — which is the Persian dynastic policy, — have hated, and at last destroyed, the few nobles of their empire; and capricious and cruel as they have been, have often shown a power of steadily upholding a great servant such as we all attribute to the founder of the new German empire. This equality, this chance of a career of great opportunities, great renown, and great luxury, brings to Constantinople a crowd of intriguers, some of them matchless villains; but it also brings a great crowd of able and unscrupulous men, who understand how to "govern" in the Turkish sense, and who have constantly succeeded in restoring a dominion which seemed hopelessly broken up. Every pasha is a despot, an able despot is soon felt, and he has in carrying out the method of Turkish government, which is simply the old Tartar method of stamping out resistance, an advantage over Europeans which is the third cause of the continuance of the Ottoman empire. He is tormented with no hesitations in applying force as a cure for all things. The man who resists is to die, or purchase life by submission. — MEREDITH TOWNSEND in "Asia and Europe."

X. SOCIAL, MORAL AND RELIGIOUS CONDITIONS

THE moral and religious condition of the people of Turkey, especially the non-Moslems, was, and still is, without a parallel in any country in the world.

Since Mohammedanism never encourages progress and education, and since the principles of Moslem rule in all countries and in all times have been based upon force, ignorance and fanaticism, it is not difficult to judge of the condition of these subject peoples, especially after many generations of oppression.

The most of the races that refused to embrace Islam and elected to pay a regular tribute for the privilege of continuing to live, were Christians, such as the Copts of Egypt, the Syrian Christians of Syria, the Jacobites of Mesopotamia, the Armenians of Armenia and sections of northern Syria and Asia Minor, the Greeks of Asia Minor, and the Bulgarians of European Turkey. While all these were Christians by profession, they had no ecclesiastical relations with each other. Each race and Church stood by itself, entirely independent of all the rest, fostering no sympathy the one with the other except in a common cause against a dominant race.

Under Moslem rule all education among the so-called Rayas was discouraged, and some of the Moslem customs, like the veiling of their women, were adopted. The low estimate placed upon womanhood by the conquerors was accepted in a measure by these races, and some of the worst of the vices of the Moslems became common among the Christians.

With these surroundings, the Christianity of the earlier days so deteriorated that little remained except the name and the outward observances of the Church. Because of the absence of modern literature and general education, the spoken language of the common people changed to such a degree that the Bible and the rituals of the Church in the ancient language in which they were written became an unknown tongue to the masses. Their religion became a religion of form, and the Bible a closed and sealed book. Surrounded as they were by all the vices of a Moslem society, dominated by Moslem rulers, the character of the Christianity among them did not attract their Mohammedan neighbors, while there was no hope for reform from within.

Jealousies and discords sprang up between the Christians of various sects whenever they came into contact, like that between the Greeks and Bulgarians in Macedonia, and the Greeks and Armenians in Asia Minor, and the Syrians and Armenians in northern Syria. The reigning sultans have not been slow to note these jealousies and to take advantage of them in dealing with the various sects. Had the Christians of Turkey during the last century been united, they might have accomplished much by way of securing privileges for themselves. But even the people of a single national Church have not been able to agree upon many important questions, so that the sultan and his subordinates have not found it hard to control these superior races, superior in themselves in many respects to their masters. If any one seemed to be giving more trouble than usual, methods were found to divide still more, and so weaken and subdue them. The same methods have been constantly employed with the various religious bodies of his empire that have been successfully used with the Euro-

SOCIAL, MORAL AND RELIGIOUS CONDITIONS

pean nations who have caused him trouble by interfering with his peculiar views of government or unjust methods of administration. He has usually succeeded in playing off the jealousies and cupidity of one against another so that concerted action became impossible and he has been left to work his own will in his own way. While the sultan has learned cunning by these conditions and gained no little advantage to himself, neither the subject Christian races of his empire nor the European nations outside have seemed to learn a lesson which is of service to them in changing existing conditions.

Under these circumstances, religion to most of the people of the country became but a form and a mark of nationality. No conversion, in the ordinary sense of the word, was required for admission to the Greek, Armenian, Bulgarian, or any of the Oriental Churches. All children were baptized in infancy and so grew up within the Church, with no religious instruction except as to fast and feast days and the proper forms to be employed in the ritual observed in the Churches. In all services the language used was no more understood by the people as a whole than Latin would be comprehended by an ordinary country audience in England or America. There was no educational or moral test for the priests except that they should be able to pronounce the words of the regular Church services and find the proper places from which to read. The writer once asked an Armenian priest where he studied. He said he was a baker and when he decided to become a priest he went to a monastery and studied for forty days. That comprised all of his schooling, except that he knew how to read simple narrative when he began. I asked him if he understood the ritual and the Scriptures that he read. He replied, " How should I know? This is the ancient Armenian." Even as late as fifteen years ago it would have been difficult to find a Christian priest of any kind or class in the interior districts who clearly understood the ritual of the Church or the Scripture read in the service. Ordinarily the selection of priests was not based upon special ability, education, or moral worth. There were, of course, noble exceptions to this most general rule.

The priests being such, and some of them most grossly ignorant and unfit, and there being in the Churches no religious instruction, it is easy to understand how the moral tone of these Oriental Churches sank rapidly under the rule of the Turk, with no power in themselves to rise above these conditions and institute a reform. A Church without a Bible, with an ignorant priesthood, with a ritual beautiful in itself but dead to the people, with no religious instruction and no test for church-membership, could not be expected in any land or in any age to keep itself unspotted from the world. Under these conditions Christianity came to be largely a name and the practises of religion only a form.

The resisting power of the Oriental Churches in Turkey was largely vitiated by the lack of the true spirit of Christianity within. At the same time, it was surrounded by evil influences and by open persecutions heavy to bear even by a living, vitalized Church. The pressure of the Mohammedans, both individually and as a government, was directed to force all professing Christians to abandon their ancestral faith and become Moslems. The heavy hand of the government was constantly upon them, while faithful Moslems were not slow to let the persecuted ones know that, should they become Mohammedans, their burdens would become lighter. Under these conditions there has constantly been more or less apostatizing from Christian-

SOCIAL, MORAL AND RELIGIOUS CONDITIONS

ity. In times of unusual persecution the number of these has increased.

At the same time, in order to avoid attention and thereby avert conflict, the Christians, in many cases, conformed to the outward practises of their Moslem masters. Their women veiled themselves when in public and covered their mouths at all times. Efforts to provide a general education for their children were largely abandoned and widespread illiteracy prevailed. The vices of the Mohammedans, some of them the vilest known to men, were practised by many of the Christians, and falsehood was so common that truth came to be almost a curiosity. To cheat or deceive a Turk was considered in itself almost a Christian virtue. In the conflict with Islam, Christianity, in its ignorance, was driven to the wall and lost nearly everything except its ancient Bible and most excellent ritual, with houses of worship, a hierarchy and a form to which it adhered with most commendable tenacity.

These untoward conditions were aggravated by the fact that, in Turkey, the Church came to be a political organization, presided over by an appointee of the sultan, who was capable of being dismissed by him if he chose to exercise his power. Each Church with its political patriarch at Constantinople constituted a little state within a state. Every Church represented a separate race or nation whose rights within the empire were vested in the rights of the Church, directed by the patriarch. At the patriarchate were recorded — and it is true to-day — all births, marriages and deaths. Individual existence in the empire was recognized only through the Church. The Christian's sole representative at Constantinople to speak for him in case of injustice, or to secure a privilege, or to obtain his legal rights, was the patriarch of his own peculiar Church.

The political organization extended down through the different provinces and included in its last analysis each individual church. Under the injustice endured by the Christians of Turkey during the past five hundred years, it is most natural that not a few of the members of the Church, if not a great majority, should look upon the organization, not primarily as a spiritual temple, but as a means of securing redress for wrongs suffered, or for obtaining privileges from the Porte. Under the laws of Turkey the Church must exercise political functions. Under the practise of the people, it came to be primarily political, the spiritual being relegated to the background.

General education never existed in that country, but under the sway of the Moslem all education was discouraged. The schools of the Moslems consisted of classes in reading the Koran in Arabic, accompanied by traditional stories of Mohammed and comments upon his teachings. Among the Christians there was little except the instruction of a few youths in monasterial schools where men were trained for Church orders. It is true that now and then among the Greeks and Armenians some bright and inquiring mind far exceeded the ordinary bounds of indigenous scholarship and became conspicuous for learning. But these were rare exceptions. The masses of the people of all classes and religions were in gross ignorance. Even within the last twenty-five years the writer has been in many Armenian villages in which not a person except the priest knew how to read and write, and even his accomplishments ceased with the bare ability to read the ritual of the Church. A leading priest once asked a student who had studied one year in a mission school, " What remains for you to learn after studying an entire year? " Under such a leadership in the Church, and with open opposition to

SOCIAL, MORAL AND RELIGIOUS CONDITIONS

general education among the Turks, it is not surprising that ignorance among the masses became almost universal, with little or no impulse to change.

If the above is true with reference to the education of the men, what could be expected for the girls and women? It is natural that, among the Mohammedans, who accord to women a low place in society and religion, it should have come to be believed in wide areas in the interior of Turkey that women were incapable of learning to read. Among them the vital question calling for early discussion was not, "Shall education be afforded to girls?" but it was, "Can girls learn to read?" This question has been hotly discussed within the last fifty years in the interior of Turkey, with the missionary contending that they can, while leading men of the country have contended with vehemence that the idea was too preposterous to consider. Conviction came only by actual demonstration.

Under such circumstances it is not difficult to imagine the general conditions of society and the deplorable life of the Church. These conditions were more or less modified in the large coast cities like Constantinople and Smyrna, but even in these places, while more educated men were found than in the interior, there was dense ignorance among the masses, and no provision for the education of girls. The entire empire had few newspapers or periodicals of any kind in any language, and the state of education stimulated the production of no great literature, even had there been those capable of producing it. The beginning of the nineteenth century, apart from the revival of learning among the Greeks of the West, may be called the dark age for literature, learning, and religion in the Turkish empire.

Constantinople and Syria were the two centers for Christian work in Turkey among the Oriental churches, because these were the centers of control for all of these churches. The chief patriarch resided at the Porte and was in close touch with his majesty the sultan, while the secondary patriarch resided at Jerusalem, cooperating with his superior at the capital. These churches could best be reached and influenced for evangelical Christianity from the same points.

Missionaries were sent to the ancient churches, not to attack them either in their doctrines or in their practises, but to cooperate with their leaders in organizing a system of education and in creating a sentiment that should demand for the Church an educated and morally upright clergy. It was expected that the Church would accept the modern version of its own Scriptures and encourage its circulation among the people. For the best conduct of a work of this character, the missionaries needed to be in close contact with the centers of ecclesiastical power in all of these churches, that from them the ordinary lines of communication might be utilized in reaching the remote interior districts.

In order that misunderstandings may be cleared up, it should be stated here that missionaries to the Armenians and Greeks were not sent to divide the churches or to separate out those who should accept education and read the Bible in the vernacular. Their one supreme endeavor was to help the Armenians and Greeks work out a quiet but genuine reform in their respective churches. The missionaries made no attacks upon the churches, their customs, or beliefs, but strove by positive, quiet effort to show the leaders how much they lacked and to help them bring about the necessary changes.

For twenty-six years this quiet work went on with no separation, in accordance with the desire of the mission-

SOCIAL, MORAL AND RELIGIOUS CONDITIONS

aries, as well as in harmony with the purposes of the Board. When the separation did come, it was in spite of every effort of the missionaries to prevent it. For the successful accomplishment of such a purpose only the centers of ecclesiastical power and influence were available. Only their own leaders could be expected to inaugurate and carry into execution a reform movement which would permeate the Church throughout the empire.

CHRISTIANITY AND ISLAM

THE mind of the true Eastern is at once lethargic and suspicious; he does not want to be reformed, and he is convinced that, if the European wishes to reform him, the desire springs from sentiments which bode him no good. Moreover, his conservatism is due to an instinct of self-preservation, and to a dim perception that, if he allows himself to be even slightly reformed, all the things to which he attaches importance will be not merely changed in this or that particular, but will rather be swept off the face of the earth. Perhaps he is not far wrong. Although there are many highly educated gentlemen who profess the Moslem religion, it has yet to be proved that Islam can assimilate civilization without succumbing in the process. It is, indeed, not improbable that, in its passage through the European crucible, many of the distinctive features of Islam, the good alike with the bad, will be volatilized, and that it will eventually issue forth in a form scarcely capable of recognition. "The Egyptians," Moses said, "whom ye have seen to-day, ye shall see them again no more for ever." The prophecy may be approaching fulfilment in a sense different from that in which it was addressed to the Israelites.

Look, moreover, not only to the spirit of the lawgivers, but to the general principles on which the laws are based. The tendency in all civilized European States is to separate religious from civil laws. In Moslem States, on the other hand, religious and civil laws are inextricably interwoven.

Look to the consequences which result from the degradation of women in Mohammedan countries. In respect to two points, both of which are of vital importance, there is a radical difference between the position of Moslem women and that of their European sisters. In the first place, the face of the Moslem woman is veiled when she appears in public. She lives a life of seclusion. The face of the European woman is exposed to view in public. The only restraints placed on her movements are those dictated by her own sense of propriety. In the second place, the East is polygamous, the West is monogamous.

It cannot be doubted that the seclusion of women exercises a baneful effect on Eastern society. The arguments on this subject are, indeed, so commonplace that it is unnecessary to dwell on them. It will be sufficient to say that seclusion, by confining the sphere of woman's interest to a very limited horizon, cramps the intellect and withers the mental development of one half of the population in Moslem countries. An Englishwoman asked an Egyptian lady how she passed her time. "I sit on this sofa," she answered, "and when I am tired, I cross over and sit on that." Moreover, inasmuch as women, in their capacities as wives and mothers, exercise a great influence over the characters of their husbands and sons, it is obvious that the seclusion of women must produce a deteriorating effect on the male population, in whose presumed interests the custom was originally established, and is still maintained. — LORD CROMER in "Modern Egypt."

XI. CHRISTIANITY AND ISLAM

FROM the day of its inception until the beginning of the last century, Mohammedanism never came into close, continuous contact with a pure Christianity. Its very beginning was a protest against a Christianity that, in its worship, had all the appearance, at least, of idolatry. The Mohammedan leaders then, as well as in subsequent generations, saw nothing in Christians which made them believe that Christianity could be better than their own religion. The Christianity with which Islam was in conflict was not such a manifestation in the lives and practises of its followers as to compel the intellectual approval of Moslems or even to command their attention. All the churches of Syria, Armenia, and Asia Minor had become worldly and formal, from which had departed the gentle spirit of their Lord, who exalted meekness, truth, purity, and righteousness. As the Mohammedans passed on towards the north and west in their victorious progress, not once did they encounter the strength of Christianity displayed in quiet meekness and forgiving love. In Europe they met the Church in arms and saw in it nothing to compel their respect.

Wherever Mohammedanism has penetrated, it has not come into vital touch with living Christianity. All that the Mohammedan knew of the practical teaching of Jesus Christ, up to the beginning of the last century, he had obtained from observing the Christians whom he conquered and controlled. It is no wonder that he concluded that his own religion was superior, when he saw the intemperance of even the leaders in the Church, and when he took note of what seemed to him to be the worship of pictures and idols. He could not see that the Christian was more truthful, or honest, or pure, than himself; hence he naturally concluded that the Christian religion was no better at least than his own faith.

A traveler in the interior of the empire, and putting up at a caravansary kept by a Mohammedan, asked him if it would be safe to leave his luggage in the outer court. The Mohammedan replied with great earnestness, "Certainly it will be safe, for there is not a Christian living within a three hours' journey of here." This incident reveals the opinion of at least one Moslem regarding the power of Christianity to make men honest.

The Mohammedans have never had an adequate opportunity of knowing Jesus Christ as Redeemer and Lord and of becoming his true disciples. They have never seen the true Christ in the face and life of his followers. They have had only a distorted vision of him, dwarfed and disfigured and marred, and in that vision they have seen no form of comeliness and no beauty that they should desire him. It is only in comparatively recent years that an effort has been made to bring to the attention of Islam the fruits of the true Christian life. It is not possible nor is it expected that the experiences and prejudices of twelve hundred years will be overcome in a single generation or even in a century. Such deep-seated convictions can be changed only by prolonged fasting, prayer, and sacrifice. Modern missions in Turkey are an attempt to show to all in that country what true Christianity means in the individual, in the family, and in society. It is not an attempt to convince the Mohammedan by argument that Mohammed is the false prophet and that Jesus Christ is God. Such an attempt would result only in failure. The Mohammedan must be made to see in the lives of the true followers of Jesus that which will give him a clear vision of the Son of man, and lead him to cry out, " My Lord and my God." I repeat, Mohammedanism has never yet had an opportunity to accept Christ and that we may not expect it to become Christian until the Christian world has demonstrated to it the beauty, love, purity, and power of the true Christian life.

These facts regarding Turkey and the various peoples who comprise its population were not fully known to the early missionaries nor to the officers of the Mission Boards. The country was largely unexplored and the vast interior was almost a *terra incognita*. Mohammedanism was vaguely understood. There was a clear knowledge of the conditions and needs of the Greek Church, but the Armenians and the other races in the remoter interior were but partially understood and only by a few. The most of our knowledge of Arabia, Syria, Eastern Turkey, and the interior of Asia Minor, the customs, beliefs, and lives of the people who dwell there, is the heritage which has come to us from the investigations and reports of missionaries who have traversed in every direction all parts of the country, except sections of Arabia. Many of these, by living among the people for a generation and mastering their language, have been able to speak with the highest authority upon what they have seen and known. We are approaching this question, not with the doubtful knowledge or even gross ignorance of eighty years ago, but with all the light that has come to us from fourscore years of mission operations which now cover practically the entire country.

Never in the history of modern missions has a more difficult and complicated work been undertaken. The questions which entered into the mission problems of the Turkish empire were legion, assuming new phases at every turn and every phase presenting a new difficulty. The one dominant note that runs through it all is the fact of Mohammedan rule. This fact in all its length and breadth must be taken into consideration. Add to this the antiquity of the old churches, the form of Christianity, from which the spirit has fled, the race hatreds, the poverty of the country, the uncertainty of everything that pertains to the government, except that it never fails to be superlatively bad, the conviction of the Moslems that they have seen true Christianity and know it to be as bad as their own government, and we have a few of the difficulties which confronted the early missionaries. On the other hand, there were the encouraging features of the reverence of the Oriental churches, all of them, for the Holy Scriptures, their allegiance to the Church, and their respect for ecclesiastics, to which must be added their superior intelligence, eagerness to learn, and capability for great advancement. Surely Turkey presented a varied scene marked by high lights and dark shadows. Without hesitation, men and women of unusual intellectual and spiritual capacity and breadth, and of indomitable courage, entered this country to win it for Christ and for Christian civilization.

EARLY PIONEERING AND EXPLORATIONS

THE elevating influence of the missionaries in Turkey cannot be overestimated. It is the most hopeful of all the influences which are at work in the empire to-day. Most people at home think of the missionary as a propagandist whose chief endeavor is to win converts to his creed, but on the field he appears as a very different character; he is an educator, a physician, a scientist, a peacemaker, a neighbor, and an example of civilized living. Judged by the numbers added to Protestant churches from the population of the Turkish empire, missions there might be counted a failure, or, at the most, but a partial success; but the making of Protestants is the smallest part of a missionary's work. 1. The missionary elevates the whole standard of Christian living and thinking. There are in Turkey churches hoary with age — Greek, Armenian, Syrian — in which ignorance, barbarism, superstition, and low morality hold sway. To retain their members in the face of the missionary, these churches find intelligence, purity, spirituality, and civilization necessary, and have been greatly elevated by missionary enterprise. 2. In countries like Turkey, where medical skill is beyond the reach of the mass of the people, the preventable suffering and death are appalling. How eagerly the villagers bring their sick to any stranger in the hope that he may be a physician, almost every traveler can testify. The brightest spots in the country are the missionary medical centers, where untold sufferings are allayed. These range all the way from the village dispensary to the Medical College at Beirut, where one of the world's best surgeons not only helps the suffering, but teaches others to do it too. 3. The most important phase of missionary work in Turkey is, however, the educational. From humble schools scattered widely through the villages to colleges like Robert College and the Syrian Protestant College at Beirut (which are the fruit of missionary enterprise) most successful efforts are being made, by broad-minded, undenominational methods, to train the young to think, and to induct them into modern science and civilization. The effect of this is already widely apparent, and it is clear that if the day ever comes when Turkey is able to take her place among the nations as a state which appreciates the laws of humanity sufficiently to be trusted, as Japan is now trusted, to control the lives and property of foreigners resident within her limits, it will be because of the civilizing influence of these educational institutions, combined with the lessons in integrity taught by the missionaries' simple Christian lives. Apart from their work for Turkey, the missionaries have contributed much to science. Archæology owes them large debts in every part of the empire, and, to mention no other fields, the only authoritative work on the botany of Syria is by a missionary. The missionaries are in my opinion working more directly than any other class of men to complete the social evolution of mankind, and to make possible the peaceable federation of the world. — GEORGE A. BARTON, PH.D., Professor of Semitic Languages in Bryn Mawr College, Director of the American School of Oriental Study and Research in Palestine, 1902–1903.

XII. EARLY PIONEERING AND EXPLORATIONS

IT was no light task to plant missions in a country so little known and extensive as was the Turkish empire at the beginning of the last century. Of the races which made up its large population little was understood except a general knowledge of the Jews and Greeks, and there was much less information regarding the Turks. In accordance with the policy already adopted by the American Board, the early missionaries were sent out to investigate and explore before deciding upon the location of missions and stations and before fixing the exact nature and methods of work.

The instructions given the earlier missionaries to Turkey seldom failed to emphasize the importance of fully examining the different parts of the country and becoming acquainted with the character, beliefs, and characteristics of the different races and peoples which comprise its population. In some cases particular unexplored regions were named as demanding immediate attention. All the early missionaries were directed to report to headquarters, in full detail, the results of their researches and observations.

In the instructions given in 1819 to Pliny Fisk and Levi Parsons, the first missionaries appointed to Turkey, the following passage occurs:

"You will survey with earnest attention the various tribes and classes which dwell in that land and in the surrounding countries. The two grand inquiries ever present in your minds will be, 'What good can be done?' and 'By what means?' What can be done for the Jews? What for the pagans? What for the Mohammedans? What for the Christians? What for the people in Palestine? What for those in Egypt, in Syria, in Armenia, in other countries to which your inquiry may be extended?"

This single quotation demonstrates the spirit of them all, and reveals the deliberate and far-seeing policy of the Board in inaugurating its missions in Turkey as well as in other countries. Men of the highest ability and broadest vision were selected for missionary appointment and upon them was placed the responsibility of selecting the location of the missions and stations, and deciding the policy and methods of work.

The archives of the Board are rich with the early reports of those first missionaries, who explored with fearlessness and zeal, and observed with discriminating care and precision. They were conscious of the fact that much in the future depended upon the thoroughness of their work and the accuracy and fulness of their reports.

Messrs. Fisk and Parsons landed at Smyrna early in 1820 and at once began the study of modern Greek. They explored the sites of the seven churches of the Apocalypse and noted their conditions and needs. Careful and minute journals were kept of all their labors and observations. In order to facilitate the work of exploration, Mr. Parsons went on alone to Palestine, where he arrived in February, 1821. One of his chief objects there was to get into touch with the Christian pilgrims who flock to the holy city in great numbers. The Greek revolution drove him back to Smyrna after several tours in Palestine, and from there he went to Alexandria, Egypt, where he died Feb. 10, 1822. Mr. Fisk was joined by Jonas King, who left his studies in Oriental literature at Paris for that purpose, and early in

EARLY PIONEERING AND EXPLORATIONS

January, 1823, the two set out for Jerusalem by way of Alexandria and Cairo. They ascended the Nile as far as Thebes, distributing everywhere Bibles and tracts in Arabic. With a caravan made up of Turks, Arabs, Greeks, and Armenians, they made the overland journey to Jerusalem and from there went down to Beirut upon the coast. Here they separated, Mr. King taking up his residence in the Lebanon mountains among the Druses, where he was most hospitably received, in order that he might the better study the Arabic language and the people. By this time, these men were using with much freedom Arabic, modern Greek, and Italian.

The tours of these first missionaries covered Tripoli, the Lebanon, Baalbec, Jaffa, Hebron, Damascus, Antioch, and Latakia, thus bringing them into close personal touch with the desert tribes as well as with the Druses, Maronites, Turks, Greeks, and other races. Mr. King returned to Smyrna overland from Tarsus, and Mr. Fisk died at Beirut Oct. 23, 1825, two years after the arrival there of Mr. and Mrs. William Goodell.

These pioneer operations were accompanied with great hardship and even peril. The difficulties were increased at this early period by the efforts of the Roman Catholics to drive all Protestants from Syria. In 1824 the missionaries in Jerusalem were apprehended, at the instigation of the Catholics, and brought before a Moslem judge, charged with distributing books which they declared to be neither Jewish, Moslem, nor Christian. Attacks by robbers were of no infrequent occurrence and fanatical uprisings were constantly to be expected. The Greco-Turkish war brought many personal perils and hardships, but did not result in the loss of missionary lives.

These experiences and subsequent investigations led to

the choice of Beirut as the missionary center for Syria and Palestine, contrary to the previous expectation that Jerusalem would be chosen. Jerusalem was carefully tested and its climate was found to be unfit for the permanent residence of American missionaries. Beirut was upon the sea, and at the same time in such relation to the Lebanon mountains that, during the heated time of the year, the missionaries could withdraw into the mountains without becoming entirely separated from the people and their work.

The matter of healthfulness was most wisely taken into consideration in selecting the location for permanent mission stations. Not that this was the solely decisive feature, but it was given due place in the weighing of arguments pro and con. Subsequent experience has proven that it is the poorest and most wasteful policy to permit missionaries to reside permanently in cities that are found to be unhealthy, or to plant in such places central institutions. Beirut has been occupied to the present day as the great mission center for Syria, and the wisdom of its choice eighty years ago has been abundantly justified. In selecting other stations in different parts of Turkey the same wise, careful method was followed.

During the ten years from 1820 to 1830 the explorations made in that country by missionaries of the Board were extensive, embracing, as has been stated, the site of the seven churches, the shores of the Nile as far as Thebes, the whole of Palestine, and the greater part of Syria. Cappadocia had been entered from Smyrna; while the Peloponnesus, the more important of the Ionian and Ægean Islands, as well as Tripoli and Tunis upon the north coast of Africa, had also received missionary visits. These careful and scientific investigations had brought to the attention of the Western world the religious beliefs and practises

EARLY PIONEERING AND EXPLORATIONS

and the moral condition of the Copts, the Maronite and Greek Churches, as well as the condition and needs of other races dwelling in that wide extent of territory.

Vast regions in that empire were still unexplored and peoples like the Armenians, Nestorians, Chaldeans, as well as Turks, Turkomans, Koords, and Persians, dwelt in the far east of Turkey and in Persia and about them little was known. The conditions and needs, and how best to meet these needs, could not be determined until all parts of the empire, all its peoples and their interrelations, were fairly well understood.

Owing to the Greco-Turkish war, which involved some of the European nations, it became necessary in 1828 to withdraw from Beirut, the center of the Syrian and Palestine work, to Malta, and for two years Beirut was unoccupied. Towards the close of 1828, Rev. Rufus Anderson, then Assistant Secretary of the American Board, was sent to Malta to meet and confer with the brethren and later to make personal investigations in Greece and the Levant. This conference led to the location of Mr. Bird in Beirut, and in sending Dr. Goodell to Constantinople.

At the same time the Prudential Committee decided to send Rev. Eli Smith and Rev. H. G. O. Dwight upon an extended tour of investigation across Asia Minor, Armenia, and Koordistan into Georgia and Persia. Mr. Smith had learned Arabic in Syria and was also somewhat familiar with the Turkish language, besides being an experienced traveler and a close and accurate observer. Mr. Dwight was just entering upon his missionary career and was full of energy and pluck.

These two men proceeded from Malta to Smyrna in March, 1830, and from there to Constantinople, overland, in April. Before beginning the journey, they placed themselves under the protection of a chief of the Tartars, who witnessed the seal of the Tartar guide to a document acknowledging responsibility for the safe delivery at Constantinople of the persons and property of the missionaries. Beds, bedding, clothing, cooking utensils, dishes, writing material, books, food, etc. were carried in waterproof leather bags upon the backs of horses. They clothed themselves in the flowing native dress of the country so as to attract as little annoying attention by the way as possible. They were also supplied with passports from the government and official letters of introduction.

While travelers had repeatedly penetrated the regions to which they were to go, none had made careful, scientific investigation of the people and of the religious and moral conditions. There was not even a map in existence upon which dependence could be placed.

After obtaining at Smyrna and Constantinople all the information possible regarding the Armenians and the country through which they were to pass, these two missionary explorers set out from the latter place on the twenty-first of May, 1830, under their Tartar guide, for the remote interior of the country. The carefully kept journal of this memorable tour is a classic of its kind. Later accounts and fuller knowledge of the region traversed by them and of the people they met give occasion for little change in the story they told to bring it up to date.

At Tocat they visited the grave of Henry Martyn who gave up his life there eighteen years before. On the thirteenth of June they entered the city of Erzerum and found it in the possession of the Russians and the headquarters of their army. The most of the Armenian population had fled. After remaining there for a few days, they pushed on east-

EARLY PIONEERING AND EXPLORATIONS

ward, creating astonishment wherever they went. Their knowledge of Turkish made it possible for them to converse freely with the people, while all were puzzled to explain the fact that their own language was known by foreigners from beyond the sea. None of the inhabitants could understand the purpose of their inquiries, for to all classes a mission solely for the sake of the people was incomprehensible. From here they faced still eastward, visiting Kars, where they met large numbers of Armenians. They continued on through Tiflis, Shoosha, Nakhchevan, Echmiadzin, and Khoy, a distance from Constantinople of more than fifteen hundred miles. When they arrived at Shoosha in the middle of August they were nearly worn out with the extreme fatigue of a journey, in itself most trying, while accommodations at night were often unfit even for a horse. They were also in the midst of cholera which had recently carried off over seventy thousand people.

They passed two and a half months in Shoosha with some German missionaries, which gave an opportunity to recuperate and study more closely the people, country, and languages. On the way to Tabriz, Persia, Mr. Smith was taken seriously ill when seventy miles from the city. Had it not been for the prompt and kindly response of the gentlemen of the English embassy at Tabriz it is doubtful whether he would have survived to reach the city.

Hitherto they had been studying the Armenian especially. At Tabriz they were in contact with the Nestorians, to investigate and report upon whom a special commission had been given them. They were here nearly two months, and then passed on to Salmas, Persia, where they came in contact with the Chaldeans, a class of Nestorians who became Roman Catholics two hundred and fifty years before. From Salmas they continued to Urumia, still in Persia, and were warmly received by the Nestorian leaders.

They returned by way of Erzerum and Trebizond, taking ship from there to Constantinople and Malta, arriving at the latter place July 2, 1831, after an absence of fifteen and a half months. In that time they had traveled over one thousand miles by water and twenty-five hundred miles by horse through a wild country beset with robbers and perils of every kind. Except when entertained by missionaries or representatives of foreign governments, a rare occurrence upon all this journey, they were compelled to occupy Oriental stables or even worse places as caravansaries and endure multifarious privations and hardships. They returned well, bringing a rich store of accurate knowledge regarding the country, people, and religions, which later proved to be of inestimable value in planting missions in all those regions. Their "Researches," consisting almost entirely of the journals they kept, cover every phase of the life and customs of the people and the conditions of the country. These were printed in two volumes, aggregating nearly seven hundred pages, and for their scientific value to the student of races, religions, geography, and language were at once recognized to be a classic. By this tour and the publication of their "Researches in Armenia," all that region was opened to the world as a proper field of operation for the Christian missionary.

As a direct result of the work of Messrs. Smith and Dwight, Mr. Perkins was sent to Tabriz in September, 1833, but owing to the unusual difficulties of the way, among which were various warring tribes of Koords, he did not arrive until nearly a year after leaving Boston. In November, 1835, he with Dr. Grant removed from

EARLY PIONEERING AND EXPLORATIONS

Tabriz to Urumia, and both these places have been the seat of mission work since. In 1835 Trebizond was occupied as a mission station, and four years later missionaries were located in Erzerum. Trebizond is upon the Black Sea and was the port of entry for all that part of the country. It is at the terminus of the great caravan route from Persia to the West, and ever since Xenophon took ship there for Constantinople, with his retreating ten thousand, has held an important place among the ports upon the coast. Erzerum is a week's journey inland upon the caravan route to Persia and is one of the most important cities in Eastern Turkey. It is situated upon a high plateau nearly six thousand feet above the sea and in the midst of a large population of Armenians, Turks, and Koords.

Dr. Asahel Grant was appointed a missionary in 1835 with the expectation that he would go to Persia. He proceeded to Urumia by way of Trebizond, Erzerum, and Tabriz. It was expected that Dr. Grant, the first missionary physician to enter that country, would investigate the conditions and needs of the mountain Nestorians who occupy the high lands of Eastern Turkey and western Persia. His allotted task demanded extensive journeys amid the wildest, least known, and most dangerous portions of the Ottoman empire. In addition to repeated tours up and down the country, his most important explorations were made in Koordistan and among the head waters of the Tigris and Euphrates rivers. From 1839 to 1845 Dr. Grant visited Van, Diarbekr, Harpoot, Mardin, Mosul, and many other towns of importance, living among the people, studying their life, winning them by the depth and sincerity of his love for them, and planning to reach them by permanently organized missionary operations. Upon a part of these journeys he was accompanied by Mr. Holmes, while much of the time, except for native servants, he was alone.

They reached Diarbekr in July, 1839, and found it in a state of anarchy. Robbery and murder were the order of the day, with a general hatred of all Europeans. They withdrew to Mardin, fifty miles south in Mesopotamia, accompanied by an escort of thirty horsemen sent for their protection by the Turkish pasha. In Mardin their lives were openly threatened. Almost by a miracle were they spared, for a mob suddenly formed and killed the governor in his palace and attacked the lodgings of the missionaries, who were providentially outside the city at the time. The city gate, closed to keep them inside for slaughter, barred them out and so saved their lives.

From here Dr. Grant went on alone to Mosul, upon the Tigris, two hundred miles below Mardin, while Mr. Holmes returned to Constantinople. It is an interesting fact that the house in which he found lodging in this important city of the far interior was but a few feet from the place that was yet to be his grave.

From Mosul he started alone in the fall of the same year for an extended tour through the unexplored mountains of Koordistan. He soon came into contact with the Yezidis, who are worshipers of Satan and more friendly to the Christians than to the Moslems. He took pains to call upon the chiefs of the country and make friends with them for the sake of the missionary work yet to be developed. He found many of the Koordish chiefs inclined to be friendly.

By means of his medical skill he was able to command the respect if not the love of all. He attended professionally the emir of a large area of country in Koordistan,

EARLY PIONEERING AND EXPLORATIONS

who gave orders a few years previously for the murder of the scientist Schultz. This tour covered eight months. He was so much changed by his native dress and rough appearance that he was not recognized by his associates at Urumia upon his arrival there.

Repeated journeys were made back and forth through that country with Urumia and Mosul as points to which he occasionally returned. The work of exploration was made much more hazardous and difficult by the hostility to each other of the Nestorians, Koords, and Turks, a hostility often manifesting itself in open war. At one time Dr. Grant was charged with being an ally of the emir and again with being a Turkish spy. His great tact, absolute fearlessness, and most winning Christian character overcame all obstacles, and under the protecting hand of God preserved him from violence.

The careful journals of Dr. Grant, even though they had to be kept in absolute secrecy to prevent the arousing of suspicions, contain some of the very best information extant to-day regarding the character and conditions of these savage but sturdy people of Eastern Turkey. In nearly all that wild country to have been caught writing would probably have resulted in his immediate death. Such an act would have stamped him as a spy or necromancer, both of which were regarded as worthy of death. While Dr. Grant was still alive, and largely by him, the attention of the American Board was emphatically called to the great needs of that country, and to the possibilities of inaugurating among the mountain Nestorians a direct evangelistic work. Many of them were Roman Catholics, nominally, but a large number were not. No special plans were then made for direct work among the Koords, as attention up to that time had been directed more to the nominal Christian races. Dr. Grant, however, pleaded that a mission might be established "to Assyria and Mesopotamia" rather than to any particular sect or race.

Dr. Grant died in Mosul, April 24, 1844, after a life brief in years but long in the extent of country covered by its influence, and thereby opened to his successors for missionary operations. Mr. Layard, the well-known Assyriologist, who later traversed Koordistan, said he had heard Mussulmans speak of Dr. Grant in the highest terms of praise, while the Koords repeatedly referred to him as "the good doctor." Few missionaries have done more in so brief a time to open to the world a country filled with savage, hostile, and warring races, and thus to lay the foundation for permanent missionary occupation. At least six places visited by him subsequently became missionary stations, all of which are now maintained.

EXPLORATIONS ALONG THE UPPER EUPHRATES AND TIGRIS RIVERS

In 1850 Rev. and Mrs. Dunmore were appointed missionaries to the city of Diarbekr, which had been previously visited by Dr. Grant and others. This city, known in classic history as Amida, is an ancient walled town upon the Tigris river located at the northern extremity of Mesopotamia. It was nearly a year before they reached their destination, having stopped for a time in Aintab and Urfa to study the Turkish language. The city was hot with persecution when they arrived, so that repeatedly the life of Mr. Dunmore was in peril. He was openly refused protection by Turkish officials and so became the common prey of all who were opposed to the hated Protestants. Mr. Dunmore was bold but tactful, and succeeded

EARLY PIONEERING AND EXPLORATIONS

finally in gaining a foothold in the city, although dire persecution was meted out to those who identified themselves with him. After the work had become fairly well established there, he began explorations into the populous, prosperous, and little known regions lying to the north. He went as far as Erzerum, visiting Mardin, Arghuni, Haine, Harpoot, Arabkir and many other towns of importance — in fact including in his tours nearly every city of influence in all those extensive regions.

Near the close of 1852 he was at Harpoot, and wrote most enthusiastically of the character of the Armenians he met there, and also of the strategic location of the city. He says: " The city overlooks a vast, rich plain studded with three hundred and sixty-six villages, of from one hundred to five thousand inhabitants each, nearly all Armenians, and all within a few hours' ride of the city. It presents, therefore, the richest country and the most inviting and promising missionary field I have seen in Turkey." He went on at length to describe the people, the climate, the accessibility of the vast populations on all sides. He urgently pleaded for missionaries to occupy the city. He not only reported upon that city, but upon many other places from twenty-five to one hundred and fifty miles away, all in the same general Euphrates river basin, presenting such a glowing account of it all that within two years two new missionary families were on their way to occupy the field. It is an interesting fact that every large place visited by Mr. Dunmore became, not many years later, either the residence of missionaries or a center of Christian operations under trained native workers.

Mr. Dunmore's gentle firmness and absolute fearlessness made a profound impression upon all whom he met. He did much to prepare the minds and hearts of the people for the coming of those who followed him; as, for instance, after enduring stonings and revilings and open threats of assassination at Diarbekr, he went boldly to the Turkish governor with a complaint against a wealthy Moslem who had greatly wronged him. The governor gave little heed, and at once exonerated the Moslem. Mr. Dunmore announced his purpose to appeal to the British Embassy at Constantinople, even to make the journey in person, in order to secure justice. The governor, after some deliberation, reversed his decision and put the Moslem in prison for two days. When he was released he called upon the missionary, begged his pardon, and announced his personal friendship. A little later, another Turk threatened Mr. Dunmore's life and was put in jail for it. This seemed to be what was required in order to give the cause standing before the community, for the attitude of the Turks changed at once, and many began to inquire about the truth which the missionaries were teaching.

Wherever Mr. Dunmore went, as was also the case with Dr. Grant, the way was remarkably prepared for the missionaries who were to follow them. These men opened all Eastern Turkey to its first knowledge of Americans and for the residence of missionaries.

In the early missionary explorations no attention was given to Arabia. At that time there seems to have been little thought about the conversion of the Mohammedans, and even had there been, the other parts of the Turkish empire afforded a sufficient number upon which to begin. Arabia seems to have been considered a remote and unknown land to which no missionary turned his tours of investigation and to which no committee at home commissioned one to preach. Arabia was indeed a remote country before the Suez Canal was opened and when

EARLY PIONEERING AND EXPLORATIONS

Bombay was reached by sailing-vessels going around the south of Africa. Of the country itself little was known, and for the most part it has never come under the full control of the sultan of Turkey or of any other country. Of the six million inhabitants of Arabia not more than one million two hundred thousand are confessedly subjects of the sultan. While he lays claim to the whole country he has not been able, up to the present time, wholly to make his claims good.

In Hejaz and Yemen, regions under the sultan, no Christian is permitted to reside or travel, and in the rest of the country the ruling emirs or imams readily inflict the death penalty upon Moslems for departure from the faith. Long after the English took control of Aden, at the extreme southwestern part of the peninsula, a mission was opened there which is called the Keith-Falconer mission, and which is now carried on by the United Free Church of Scotland. In 1889 an independent interdenominational mission was opened upon the western shore of the Persian Gulf. Members of this mission have penetrated into the interior of the country and have given to the world much valuable information regarding this land of mystery and its inhabitants of ancient name and fame. This mission was adopted by the Board of the Reformed (Dutch) Church of America in 1894.

It is remarkable that this cradle of Islam, lying so close to the great highway between the West and the far East, should still remain practically untouched by modern education and the fundamental truths of Christianity. It cannot long maintain its barriers against the onrush of modern thought and life.

ESTABLISHED CENTERS

So far as Americans are concerned, the missionary work in European Turkey and Asia Minor is and long has been almost exclusively in the hands of the American Board. In no part of the world has that Board or any Board had abler or more devoted representatives to preach the gospel, to conduct schools and colleges or to establish and administer hospitals. Their original aim was to infuse new life into the native Armenian and Greek churches, to rescue them from mere formalism, and to imbue them with the spirit of a pure and active Christianity. Circumstances compelled them in due time to organize independent churches on which the old churches at first looked with unfriendly eyes. But of late years in many places a more friendly and sympathetic spirit has been manifested towards them by the clergy of the old order, and the life of some of the native churches has been quickened by the example of the missionary churches.

The excellence of our schools has been so manifest that its stimulating effect has been felt by not only the Armenian and Greek schools, but also by the Turkish schools.

The medical work of our missionary physicians has also widely commended itself to men of all faiths and has awakened a decided interest not only in the religion which so humanely brings its generous hospital treatment to all who desire it, but also in the rational system of medicine and surgery which it illustrates. Even the Mohammedans who are generally inaccessible to the approaches of our missionaries cannot but have some appreciation of the benevolent and Christlike work of our physicians.

Wherever an American mission is established, there is a center of alert, enterprising American life, whose influence in a hundred ways is felt even by the lethargic Oriental life. — PROF. JAMES B. ANGELL, LL. D., University of Michigan, Ex. U. S. Minister to Turkey and China.

XIII. ESTABLISHED CENTERS

SMYRNA was the first station of the Levant occupied by American missionaries. This was an important city of Turkey and, until Constantinople was better understood, was considered the most important city to hold as the central station of the missions to Turkey. Since 1820 this place has been one of the stations of the American Board and the residence of one or more missionary families. This was regarded as a good starting-point for work among the Greeks, as well as other races centering there in large numbers.

Beirut, after an attempt to locate in Jerusalem, was occupied as a station three years later. While the original plans for work in Syria had the Jews most distinctly in mind, attention was quickly diverted to other races more alert and promising.

It was inevitable that Constantinople should early become the headquarters of missions in the Ottoman empire as it was the political capital and commercial metropolis. The climate is healthy, and being partly in Europe and partly in Asia, the city partakes in part of the character of both continents.

There was also another strong reason for making Constantinople the headquarters of work in Turkey, namely, the fact that it was the headquarters of every important religious sect in the empire. Opposition to mission work must emanate from that center and difficulties could best be overcome right at their beginning. As it was also the seat of government from which governors and civil officers were sent to every part of the empire, this made it still more important that a strong mission force should reside here, in order that these men should not receive the impression that Christian missionaries are advancing upon the empire only through remote interior districts. The capital was occupied as a mission station of the Board in 1831, and has since been the base of operations for the work of the American Board in the country. Tours of exploration made in Asia Minor and into Koordistan and Persia started from this center.

Preliminary explorations had been made by various scientific societies, as for instance that of John M. Parker, F.G.S., F.R.G.S., under the auspices of the Royal Geographical Society and the Society for Promoting Christian Knowledge, in 1839–40. They went overland from Constantinople to Cæsarea, Malatia, Diarbekr, Mosul, Koordistan, Bitlis, Marash, Erzerum, Trebizond, and thence back to Constantinople. The report of this extended tour through Asia Minor, northern Mesopotamia, Koordistan, and Armenia, published in two volumes, under the title "Travels and Researches in Asia Minor, Mesopotamia, Chaldea, and Armenia," was of great value to the missionaries in planning their locations. These researches were made largely from the purely scientific standpoint and in some cases needed to be supplemented by missionary observations.

The establishing of mission locations over the vast areas of Asiatic and European Turkey was not hastily carried out. The country was well mapped and explored before the stations were opened, and then only such places were chosen as promised to be central to large populations and healthful for missionary residences. The policy seems to have been early adopted to set the stations far apart, with two or more missionary families in each of

ESTABLISHED CENTERS

them. The success of this plan has proven its wisdom, and even now the tendency is to greater consolidation in important centers rather than to a scattering of forces.

A few, and but a few, places early opened as stations were later abandoned. Three of these were Mosul, Diarbekr, and Arabkir. The former place proved to be exceedingly unhealthy and was made an outstation of Mardin, while the two latter places were within one hundred miles of Harpoot and were made outstations. The carefulness and foresight with which the early stations were chosen are proved by the test of over fifty years of successful occupancy.

Trebizond, upon the southern shore of the Black Sea towards its eastern extremity, was occupied as a station, as already stated, in 1835. It is a large city of great influence, with a Greek, Armenian, and Turkish population.

In 1839 a missionary family was sent to Erzerum, one hundred and ten miles into the interior to the southeast of Trebizond. As soon as these stations were opened they became the centers of exploration for securing and forwarding information to the headquarters of the missions in Constantinople and to the Board in Boston.

Aintab was opened in what was then called " Southern Armenia," in 1849, and became the center for operations upon a large population dwelling in northern Syria, extending from Urfa on the east into the Tarsus mountains upon the west, and including the important cities of Marash, opened in 1855, Adana, Aleppo, Tarsus, Hadjin, Antioch, Kilis, and many other towns of less importance. Later this became the center of what came to be known as the Central Turkey Mission. This region is approached from the Mediterranean and is inhabited chiefly by Armenians and Turks. In this section of country the Armenians have lost, for the most part, their native tongue, and speak only the Turkish language. As the Koords and more savage races live in remote regions, the people have not endured the persecution here that their brethren in the north and east have been called upon to pass through.

In 1850 an investigation of the condition of the Jews in Salonica was made, which resulted in the opening of that station for work, especially among the Jews. There seems to have been no thought of reaching from that station any other races. They found the Jews there extremely ignorant, and divided between the Rabbinicals and the Mohammedans. The unhealthy condition of the city led in 1859 to the transfer of the station to Smyrna.

The more interior stations, like Marsovan, Cæsarea, Sivas, Harpoot and Bitlis, were occupied in the '50s, while Van, the most eastern mission station in Turkey, was made such in 1872. From Constantinople the missionaries had been gradually reaching out, Nicomedia and Brusa having been made stations in 1847 and 1848, respectively.

The languages used in these missions were the Arabic and Syrian in the Syrian field with its center at Beirut; the Turkish language in the Central Turkey region with its center at Aintab; the Armenian language in the Eastern Turkey district with its center at Harpoot; while Arabic was the language of Mardin, Mosul and Arabia, and the Greek, Armenian, Bulgarian and Turkish languages in the Western Turkey mission including Trebizond. Various plans were tried at first of grouping these various stations for purposes of control and administration. They could not all be classed together owing to the long distances separating them and the difficulties of travel in a country with no roads and no public conveyances. Finally the above outlined arrangement of the stations was adopted and each separate mission became a little republic in itself, holding its annual meeting, in which delegates from all the stations belonging to it met and legislated for it as a whole. In 1872 the European Turkey mission also became separate from the Western Turkey mission and has since been conducted as an entirely distinct organization.

The great extent of territory covered by these missions can best be understood by the fact that but few stations anywhere were less than one hundred miles apart. The nearest station to Harpoot in Eastern Turkey was distant one hundred and fifty miles, a six days' journey by the ordinary mode of conveyance. To reach some of the interior stations like Bitlis, Harpoot and Mardin required an overland journey on horseback of from three to four weeks from the Black Sea coast. Thus the country was dotted by mission stations which became at once centers for direct, aggressive, educational, philanthropic and Christian work. In no case was one opened except upon the urgent invitation of a large number of the people themselves. A station meant then, as it means to-day, a center in which missionaries reside. It was understood also that this residence was permanent, and to make this clear to all, houses for the missionaries were purchased or erected and other arrangements completed for a lifework. This fact in itself made a profound impression upon the people of all classes and religions. When it was charged that the missionary movement would prove to be short-lived, no one was able to answer the question, "What mean these residences owned by the missionaries?" Certainly, if it was the purpose to carry on only a temporary work, houses would have been leased. Another fact, which gave the appearance and impression of permanency, was that the missionaries came with their wives and set up their homes there. These two facts had much to do in giving stability and strength to the earlier work. The three men and their wives who occupied the Harpoot station in 1858 were there together in that same station until after the massacres of 1895, when owing to broken health and the destruction of their homes four of them were compelled to come to this country. Three of the six are still living, two of them at Harpoot. The policy of married missionaries permanently located in central stations and from there working together as a unit the large adjacent field, has proved itself to be a wise and efficient policy for all parts of Turkey. This policy necessitates the wide use of trained native pastors, preachers, evangelists and teachers who occupy the outstations and push the work into the remoter districts.

Each station became a social settlement, in which the Christian home was the center and from which wholesome Christian influences were exerted upon all with whom the missionaries came in contact. The plan involved the elevation and purification of the entire social fabric of the country, and, judged from our modern standpoint, no more effectual way of accomplishing this could have been devised. It is no small thing for devout philanthropists in England and the United States to give up their comfortable homes and establish their residence, as many have done and are still doing, among the downtrodden and oppressed in our great cities. It is well known, however, that this change of residence is not permanent and that, in cases of sickness, the old home and friends remain, to which re-

ESTABLISHED CENTERS

turn can be made. With those missionaries the case was different. Their homes in America were broken up. They took up their abode in the interior cities of Turkey for life. In times of sickness they remained. No friends from home visited them, and in case of their death, their bodies were buried in the soil of the land. There were their children born, and in multitudes of cases, because of the severity of the climate and the lack of proper facilities for safeguarding their health, there also were they buried. Herein lie many elements of moral strength which appear in the foreign missionary movement. It is this feature which has made a profound impression upon the races of Turkey and which is now reshaping its social system.

In 1860, after forty years of exploration and study in the Turkish empire, so far as her people and their moral and spiritual needs were concerned, missionary work had been outlined for at least five different races. Interest in the Jews had been continued, and a missionary, Dr. Schauffler, intended exclusively for work among them, had been maintained, not at Jerusalem but at Constantinople. He was working in harmony with the three English and Scottish societies, each of whom was maintaining missionaries to the Jews, with headquarters at Constantinople. The work done was quiet, exciting apparently less interest among the people of Turkey than among the organizers of societies in the United States for work among this race. Undoubtedly, during the first generation of work in the Ottoman empire, the people of the United States and England were more stirred by appeals for work among the Jews than by any other appeal which was or could be made.

The work for the Greeks was promising in Smyrna and Constantinople. Owing to Greece obtaining her freedom from the rule of the sultan, Greeks still living in Turkey were drawn away in their sympathies and interest to Greece, and the spirit of patriotism was strong in holding them to the national Church.

Among the Syrians a hold was obtained in spite of the intense opposition of the Roman Catholics who claimed all Syrians as belonging to them. The severest opposition during the first twenty-five years of mission effort in Turkey came not from the Turks but from the Roman Catholics, who did not stop at the employment of any measure which would tend to banish the printing-press and curtail the work of the Protestant missionaries.

The Mohammedans commanded early attention. They were drawn to the missionaries by the fact that no pictures or images were used in Protestant worship nor gaudy display made in any public services. Repeatedly Turks said to the missionaries, " You are like us, you are good Moslems." As acquaintance increased, interest deepened in this dominant race. Conditions were such that little directly aggressive effort could be wisely made for their immediate enlightenment. Much was done in the way of private conversation and through the preparation and publication of a Christian literature adapted to their needs.

It may be said, however, that the Armenians most completely commanded both the interest of the missionaries and the attention of the constituency at home. The most of the stations in the country were established especially for this race. They were found at every center. Even in Syria and in all of the interior stations, Armenians and Turks were the chief people with whom the missionaries constantly came in contact. Interest in Armenians was strengthened by the intense persecutions through which

ESTABLISHED CENTERS

the evangelicals passed in the early '40s, at the hand of their own ecclesiastics. They were open-minded, able, and devout, and presented a wide opportunity for sowing the seeds of intelligent belief. At that time little had been done for the Bulgarians in European Turkey and Macedonia. The more remote Asiatic field had proved to be so large and so interesting that there had been scant pause to look into the conditions and needs of the people so near at hand, occupying the southeastern corner of Europe.

Levi Parsons and Pliny Fisk, writing from Smyrna to the Board rooms in February, 1820, said, "In all the populous Catholic and Mohammedan countries on the north and south side of the Mediterranean there is not a single Protestant missionary. In all the Turkish empire, containing perhaps twenty million souls, not one missionary station is permanently occupied and but a single missionary besides ourselves." This one man did not long remain. Besides the English work among the Jews and Turks in Constantinople and Palestine, the evangelization of the Turkish empire was left from the first to the American Board. In later years the Disciples of Christ and the Seventh Day Adventists have sent a few missionaries into the country, but their work has been almost exclusively among the Protestants and has resulted only in dividing churches already organized. The Church Missionary Society of England has had some work in Bagdad, and a Scotch society in Aden and the Reformed Church of the United States has recently begun operations upon the southern coast of Arabia. With a few other minor exceptions, the Turkish empire north of Syria has been generally conceded to be the distinctive mission field of the American Board of Missions.

When the division of fields took place in 1870 between

the American Board and the newly organized Presbyterian Board of Missions, southern Syria and Persia were assigned to that Board, while the American Board retained northern Syria and all the rest of Turkey. In European Turkey the same Board is in sole charge of all the evangelical work for and among the Bulgarians south of the Balkans, the Methodist Episcopal Board of the United States having a work among the same people north of the Balkans. Thus Macedonia and Bulgaria south of the Balkans, Asia Minor, Armenia, Koordistan, northern Syria and northern Mesopotamia are left the sole field of the American Board, with the few exceptions mentioned above. This has put upon it a responsibility and placed before it an opportunity such as few mission agencies in modern times have had to face.

BEGINNINGS IN REFORM

I HAD occasion some years ago to visit a considerable part of Turkey, from Constantinople and Beirut to Mosul and Bagdad, and everywhere I paid particular attention to missionary conditions and the influence of mission work upon the people. This is a land assigned almost wholly to American Missionary Boards, and the influence is everywhere marked and excellent. The late Premier Stviloff told me in Sofia that but for young men educated by American teachers in Constantinople, Bulgaria when it became independent would have had to depend on Russians for administrative officers. He was himself, like so many other distinguished Bulgarians, a graduate of Robert College. In Syria a native physician, graduated at the Syrian Protestant College, said to me, "We say, 'After God, van Dyke.'" In the interior cities, such as Marash, Aintab, Urfa, Mardin and Diarbekr, the American schools and the large self-supporting churches were evidences of the new evangelic spirit and culture which had put new heart into those ancient seats of intellectual decay. About Harpoot there were thousands who had learned English, and hundreds have come from there to this country believing it to be a very paradise. The contrast was sad enough when I came into the towns south from Mosul where American missionary influence had not reached, and scarce any signs of intellectual or material improvement were to be found. I am convinced that the work of devoted, intelligent, broad-minded missionaries is far more effective in lifting a people out of ignorance and social decay into enlightened civilization, than all the influences of commerce or mere governmental policy. Our missionaries bring the motive of faith as the example of unselfish service which nothing else can supply. — WILLIAM HAYES WARD, LL. D., Editor "New York Independent."

XIV. BEGINNINGS IN REFORM

DURING the first generation of missionary operations in Turkey there were few tangible results except among the Armenians. The Mohammedans were by no means entirely hostile and revealed much friendliness and often open sympathy. The Jews presented almost a solid wall of stolid opposition to the effort for reform among them, while the Syrians and Greeks, under the leadership of the Roman Catholics, were often violent in their open attacks and secret plottings to thwart every attempt of the missionaries to gain a foothold in the country. The people in all the empire who seemed to have been especially prepared to receive and profit by evangelical teaching were the Armenians, who were not distinctly in mind when mission work in Turkey was first contemplated. In fact, almost nothing was then known of these people in the world at large and among the Christians of the United States who were supporting the cause of foreign missions.

While the American Board contemplated extending its missions in the Levant to the shores of the Black Sea and especially into Armenia, no mention whatever seems to have been made of the Armenians in connection with the beginning of the first " mission to Palestine."

Not long after Rev. Levi Parsons arrived at Jerusalem in 1821 and upon his first visit there, he came into contact with some Armenian pilgrims with whom he had conversation upon the subject of missions to their people and country. These expressed themselves as eager to have missionaries sent to them. Mr. Fisk at about the same time, writing to Boston from Smyrna, recommended the appointment of missionaries to Armenia. From this time the idea of work among the Armenians enlarged and deepened, although the "mission to the Jews" was kept persistently at the front.

There had been a vast deal of preparation of the Armenian people for a work of reform, emanating from sources quite outside of the Board and, in fact, considerably anterior to its organization. Somewhere about 1760, an Armenian priest, who was burning with the desire to reform the Armenian Church, appeared in Constantinople. He saw and deeply felt the gross errors of the Gregorian Church, and wrote a book exposing them. He was an educated man and seems to have been more or less familiar with the work of Martin Luther, of whose Reformation he heartily approved. He constantly referred to the Bible and to this high standard he mercilessly brought his Church and its clergy. The inconsistent life of the priests and bishops, and the gross superstitions of the people at large, greatly troubled him. He lacked, however, true spiritual enlightenment and power, and failed to see divine truth in its breadth and purity. His book was never printed, but copies were kept in various places which were brought to light and repeatedly referred to later. This effort had wide influence in revealing the errors of the Armenian Church, and did much to prepare the way for the genuine reformatory movement.

In 1813, six years before the American Board appointed its first missionary to Palestine, the British and Russian Bible Societies made strenuous efforts to provide for the Armenian people a Bible in their own tongue. An edition of an old fourth century Armenian version of the entire Bible was commenced in that year at St. Petersburg by the Russian Bible Society, and at about the same time

BEGINNINGS IN REFORM

another edition of the same Bible was put on the press by the Calcutta Auxiliary of the British and Foreign Bible Society. The Russian edition of five thousand copies was out in 1815, and the British edition of two thousand copies appeared two years later. The Russian Society issued a separate edition of two thousand copies of the Ancient Armenian New Testament.

In their report of 1814 the British and Foreign Bible Society said that the printing of the Armenian Testament had aroused much interest among the Armenians, especially those in Russia. Emperor Alexander at that time took a keen interest in the work of the Russian Bible Society and therefore the cause itself became popular among all classes. The Armenian Catholicos, the spiritual head of that Church, with residence at Etchmiadzin, now in Russia, bordering upon Armenia, was elected one of the vice-presidents of the society. He wrote a letter to its president commending the work of the society, and approving of the plan to supply his own people with the Word of God. The Armenian archbishop of Tiflis contributed six hundred roubles for that purpose.

In 1818 the British and Foreign Bible Society purchased one thousand five hundred copies of the Armenian New Testament from the Armenian Catholic College located on the Island of St. Lazarus, Venice, for distribution among the Armenians. Later, a still larger number was purchased and distributed in the same way. In 1823 the same Bible Society published at Constantinople an edition of five thousand copies of the Armenian New Testament and three thousand copies of the four Gospels alone. These books were rapidly distributed by agents of the British and Foreign Bible Society and by Mr. Connor of the Church Missionary Society, at that time in Constantinople, among the Armenians of the Trans-Caucasian provinces in Russia and in Turkey.

These facts have an important bearing upon the preparation of the Armenians for a reform movement. Hitherto, while they had the Bible in its entirety, it was mostly in manuscript form, and inaccessible to the people. These valuable copies of the Holy Scriptures were kept in the monasteries or in the larger churches, carefully guarded by the priests or other custodians, who usually were themselves unable to read or understand the writing. All the Armenians everywhere accepted the Bible as the divine and inspired Word of God.

The name of the Bible is Astvadsashoonch, or "*The breath of God.*" With joy they welcomed the printed word that could be kept in their houses, handled with their own hands, and perused at their leisure. Hitherto they had been permitted only to kiss its silver adorned covers at the close of the formal services of their churches.

It was soon found, however, that the ancient Armenian, the language of all the manuscripts of the Bible and rituals of the Old Church and also of the Bibles and Testaments recently printed, was not understood by the common, uneducated people. As the educated were few, the number of intelligent readers was greatly limited. This number was confined practically to the higher clergy, a few priests and vartabeds, and the teachers in the schools. In order to reach the common people, the Russian Bible Society issued in 1822 and 1823 a New Testament translated into Turkish and printed with the Armenian character. As a large proportion of the Armenians understood Turkish this version brought to them the Word of God.

Hitherto the Armenian ecclesiastics had made little or no opposition to the circulation of the Bible among the

BEGINNINGS IN REFORM

people, while some of the most prominent seemed to favor the work. In 1823 the agents of the British and Foreign Bible Society at Constantinople endeavored to secure the sanction of the Armenian patriarch for the printing and circulation of the New Testament in the modern, spoken Armenian tongue, the home language of most of the Armenians in Turkey. They were met with the severest opposition, and with threats of prohibiting the reading of the book if it should be issued.

Without attempting to follow the course of Bible publication, upon which depended the plan of reform for both the Armenian and Greek churches as well as for all the other races dwelling in the empire, suffice it to say that the hostility of the Armenian clergy, called forth by the publication of the modern Armenian version of the Scriptures, started a conflict, which waged throughout the country for more than a generation, as to whether that version was the true Word of God. The ancient Armenian Scriptures were translated from the Septuagint and the Latin Vulgate while the modern versions were made from the Hebrew and Greek. For this reason there were many discrepancies between the two versions which were discussed everywhere. This drove the people to a careful study of the Bible. If it could be once established that the modern version was also the "Word of God," there could be no hesitation upon the part of the Armenians in accepting it as such. This phase of the controversy passed fully forty years ago, and throughout the country this version is now accepted as *Astvadsashoonch* or the *veritable Word of God*. It was, however, for many years a vital question which commanded the attention and energy of the strongest men of the race.

The work of Bible translation and publication has continued under the patronage of the British and Foreign Bible Society and the American Bible Society until the entire Bible is now available for all Turkish, Arabic, Syrian, Persian, Armenian, Bulgarian, and Greek speaking peoples, and parts of the same are available for the Koords and Albanians. Nothing in the line of reform in Turkey has been more potent than the Word of God in the spoken languages of its many-tongued people, put up in cheap form and in convenient sizes and widely distributed in all parts of the empire. The Bible is not only welcomed by nearly all classes, but it is eagerly sought by many who are remotely informed of its contents but who are eager to investigate for themselves. It is an interesting fact that wherever the Bible, and especially the New Testament, has been most widely read, there the people have been the more determined to have modern educational facilities for their children and better prepared to welcome the better forms of Western civilization.

LEADERS, METHODS, AND ANATHEMAS

I MUST frankly confess that when I first went to Turkey I was somewhat prejudiced against the missionaries there and missionary work, to this extent: As what, I suppose, you might call a high Anglican, I looked with a certain esteem and regard upon the old churches of the East and it seemed to me theoretically that the proper method of missionary enterprise was to try to cooperate with those churches, helping them to educate and evangelize themselves. As a result of contact first with the Congregational missionaries of the A. B. C. F. M., this prejudice very speedily vanished. I found those men not only most earnest and devout Christians, but, so to speak, thoroughly Catholic and non-partisan, and I found that they had profoundly influenced for good the ancient Christian churches where they had come in contact with them and, in fact, regenerated (I think the term is not too strong) the Armenian Church. They themselves were men not only of culture and refinement and earnest religious devotion, but of broad, statesmanlike views, an unusual group.

At Constantinople I was also brought into close contact with the men and women conducting the two great colleges, Robert College at Roumelia Hissar and the Woman's College at Scutari, and had some opportunity to estimate the value of that work and its profound influence as a civilizing agent on the community at large. Later I was brought into contact with the Syrian Protestant College at Beirut, and with the Congregational and Presbyterian missionaries through Syria, and the favorable impressions made at Constantinople were confirmed and strengthened. My travels into regions touched by American missionaries, and beyond the confines of those regions, enabled me to form an estimate of the real influence of the missionaries on the country at large. It has been enormous. One thing, especially, the missionaries have given honor everywhere to the American name, so that to be known as an American almost anywhere in Turkey, is to ensure the confidence of the people. That name is the synonym of honest and disinterested service of one's fellow men. I wish that the name American carried in every country the meaning which American missionaries have caused it to bear in Turkey, and I may add in Bulgaria.

But I must not be too lengthy. I am apt to wax enthusiastic when I speak on this subject, and am sometimes afraid my language may seem extravagant. It is difficult to comprehend how such a relatively small body of men, with such a relatively small expenditure of money, has made so profound an impression on the life of the people of the empire as has been made by the American missionaries and the American schools and colleges. They have been the great means of uplift, both directly and also indirectly, in causing the establishment by other nations and by the Turks themselves, of schools and the like, thus diffusing still further education.

I wish I had time and space to speak further of the great needs of the people of Turkey which must be met, if at all, through missionary agencies and of the great opportunities which the field presents in spite of all hindrances and difficulties. — PROF. JOHN P. PETERS, D. D., ScD., Explorer.

XV. LEADERS, METHODS, AND ANATHEMAS

IT should be stated at the outset that the purpose of the American Board in its efforts for the Armenians was not to weaken the old Gregorian Church or to proselyte from it. There was no desire to form among the Armenians an evangelical or Protestant Church. There was no purpose to form any organization among them, but simply to introduce the New Testament in the spoken tongue of the people and to assist them in working out reforms in their old Church and under their own leaders.

The first missionary sent to Constantinople by the Board was the Rev. William Goodell, transferred from Beirut by way of Malta to open a mission at the capital of the empire with a view to reaching the Armenians there. In his work of translating the Bible into Armeno-Turkish at Beirut he had been ably assisted by two prominent Armenians, one a bishop and one a learned vartabed, who had fully accepted the modern Bible and were firm believers in the necessity of reform for the Armenian Church. Dr. Goodell may be called the father of the Armenian mission and the shaper of its policy. He was a man of great intellectual ability, clear spiritual insight and practical wisdom. After familiarizing himself with the situation at Constantinople he wrote:

"In almost every place individuals are found who are so far enlightened as to see and feel that their churches are abominably corrupt, and who do sincerely desire a reform. We ourselves at this place have nothing to do with the Church, its dogmas, ceremonies and superstitions, nor do we ever think of meddling with the convents, the priests, the celibacy of the clergy, etc. In fact, we stand nearly as far aloof from ecclesiastical matters as we do from political matters. We find no occasion to touch them. We direct men to their own hearts and to the Bible. Nor do we make any attempt to establish a new Church or raise up a new party. We disdain everything of the kind. We tell them frankly, 'You have sects enough among you already, and we have no design of setting up a new one, or of pulling down your churches, or drawing away members from them in order to build up our own.' No, let him who is a Greek be a Greek still, and him who is an Armenian be an Armenian still."

In another place he wrote, "The less that is said and known about our operations so much the better. A great deal can be done in a silent, harmless, inoffensive way in these countries, but nothing in a storm." Again he said, "Our kingdom is not of this world, we are building up no Church here, nor forming any ecclesiastical organization whatever."

These utterances of Dr. Goodell, which might be greatly multiplied, are enough to show the plan he had worked out for mission operations among the Oriental churches. The attitude of the officers of the Board in Boston was in full accord with this purpose and method. In a word, the aim of missions to the Oriental churches was not to organize a separate Church but to give them the Word of God in their own spoken tongue, help them to understand its teachings, and then to cooperate with them in organizing and carrying out such measures of reform as might seem wise and practicable to their own leaders. In carrying out this plan no separate meetings were begun. The only distinct religious services carried on in Constantinople by the missionaries in all these years of beginnings were private worship in English for themselves, their children, and

LEADERS, METHODS, AND ANATHEMAS

other English speaking people in the city who chose to join them. Apart from this, their time was given to personal conversation with individuals, dwelling largely upon the interpretation of the Scriptures. Men who felt they must separate from the old Church were persuaded to remain within the Church and to work there for gradual reforms. These purposes and plans were talked over freely with the patriarch, with the priests, bishops, and leaders of the Church, and met with their hearty approval. The missionaries attended the services of the old Church upon the Sabbath and on special occasions at other times, and frequently took part, as they were invited so to do. The contemplated reforms had nothing to do with the ecclesiastical systems or ritual then dominating. There was no desire to change these. The one aim was as declared in the expression frequently used, "*To build up truth.*" When truth prevails error will depart.

It was plain to all, and to none more than to the Armenian leaders, that no permanent reforms could be wrought out within the Church without schools for the education of priests. It was apparent that, so long as the ministers in the churches were for the most part untaught, ignorant, and often coarse, the Church could never be lifted from its low intellectual, moral, and spiritual plane. Because of the general ignorance of so many of the clergy, the cause of education among the Armenians had everywhere gone into decadence. Fully recognizing these conditions and needs, and at the same time aware that the situation was delicate, Dr. Goodell and his associates, instead of starting mission schools, persuaded the Greeks and the Armenians to establish schools of their own, proffering missionary assistance as it might be called for.

DAYBREAK IN TURKEY

At about the time mission work began in Turkey, the system of schools organized by Joseph Lancaster of England was attracting much attention, not only in that country but in the United States. This was a monitor system requiring few trained teachers, no text-books, and seemed to command popular interest wherever tried, and undoubtedly afforded a quick and superficial exhibit of progress in the pupils. Lancasterian schools were having a period of great popularity in Greece. They spread to Constantinople and were at once adopted by Greeks, Armenians, and Turks. These had the effect of arousing the popular mind, and awaking a desire for an education. These schools were, for the most part, religious, but not sectarian. They were not long continued by either the Turks or the Greeks, but the seed of learning fell into especially fruitful soil among the Armenians.

Another influence had been operating at the capital leading towards this same end. When Jonas King left Syria he wrote a farewell letter dwelling at length upon the needs of reform in the Oriental churches, with many Scriptural references to prove his position. An Armenian bishop, Dionysius, translated this letter into Armenian, and in 1827 a manuscript copy was sent by him to some of the more influential Armenians in Constantinople. The effect of it was remarkable. A meeting was called in the Armenian Patriarchal Church at which the letter was read and the Scriptures referred to examined. By common consent it was there agreed that the Church needed reforming. The well known school of Pashtimaljian was the direct outgrowth of that meeting. It was there decided that no Armenian priest should be ordained in Constantinople who had not completed a regular course of study in that school.

LEADERS, METHODS, AND ANATHEMAS

This school exerted a strong influence in preparing the minds of a large body of young men to receive the truth and later to become leaders in the movement towards reform. Pashtimaljian himself was an Armenian of remarkable ability and strength. He was an accurate scholar and a critical student of the Armenian language and literature, and, although a layman, was well versed in Eastern theology and Church history. He was equally accurate and thorough in his study of the Bible. His leadership was recognized by the Armenians. He was a friend of the missionaries, but for fear of exciting the suspicions of his race carried on his work independently of them. While evangelical in his beliefs and thoughts he did not, to the day of his death, in 1837, openly declare himself to be an evangelical. But up to that time there had been no break with the old Church and no persecution of those who were studying the Word of God.

In all cases where the word "Evangelical" is used in connection with the Armenians, Greeks or Syrians it refers to those who are recognized as regular readers of the New Testament in the vernacular. The "Evangelicals" among the Armenians were those who persisted in adhering to their right to read the New Testament and to follow its manifest teachings even in the face of the disapproval of their ecclesiastics. Under the fire of anathemas and persecution the word came to be applied to those who were cast out of the Gregorian Church because they would not discontinue the practise. In Turkey the word has only its original meaning, derived from the "Evangel" of Christ.

In 1833 the missionaries at Constantinople were invited to be present in the Patriarchal Church at the ordination of fifteen Armenian priests, trained in Pashtimaljian's school. These men were largely emancipated from the superstitions of the old Church and alert to the needs of radical reform. When the break between the Gregorians and the Evangelicals actually took place, several years later, the leaders of the Protestants were for the most part men who had received their training under Pashtimaljian, who was always independent of missionary supervision and who was highly esteemed and honored by the ecclesiastics of the Gregorian Church.

With all these forces at work upon this able and alert people, advanced ideas rapidly spread among all classes at the capital, and through constant intercourse with the chief cities in the interior, aroused there also the spirit of inquiry. The patriarch at Constantinople and some of the bishops in interior towns seemed in hearty accord with the revival of Biblical study and of true learning. The missionaries endeavored to have the Armenians themselves open and conduct all the schools, and ventured themselves to do anything of the kind only when they failed to get the people to act.

The steady progress of the reform movement was hindered by great fires in the city, by cholera and plague, and by civil war. Even to the present these distracting and disintegrating forces have always been present in some parts of the Turkish fields, presenting many obstacles to continuous advance.

The Roman Catholics were openly opposed to the circulation of the Bible among the people, and used their influence to check the movement for a revival of righteousness and learning. By constant effort, even in the days of Pashtimaljian, they cast suspicion upon the movement into the minds of some of the leaders among the old Church people. An anti-reform party was gradually

LEADERS, METHODS, AND ANATHEMAS

formed, led largely by uneducated ecclesiastics, who saw that if only educated men were to be ordained to the priesthood and were to exercise a leading influence in the Church, their power would soon be destroyed. They succeeded in exalting to patriarchal power in 1839 an astute and bigoted man from the interior of the country. He began at once to arrest and throw into prison some of the leading men in the evangelical movement. Some even were banished into the interior for the sole crime of reading the Bible.

The Armenian Evangelical Union, a secret organization, had in 1839 some twenty-two members. It was an organized company of intelligent, advanced thinkers, who came together to plan and pray for the reformation of their Church and of the country, and for Bible study. They carried on secret correspondence with men of enlightenment throughout the empire. None of them were separated from the Church nor did they contemplate such a step nor encourage it in others. They were planning solely for the salvation of the Gregorian Church. These unions were continued and multiplied in the country, but not as a secret society after the organization of the Protestant churches.

On the third of March, 1839, a patriarchal bull was issued by Hagopos, adjunct patriarch, forbidding the reading of all books printed or circulated by the missionaries, and all who possessed such books were ordered to deliver them up. A few days later the sympathetic and gentle patriarch Stepan was deposed and Hagopos was installed in his place. Spurred on by the same Romanists, the Greek patriarch issued a similar bull to all Greeks against the books of the missionaries. The reign of terror thus begun raged in the capital and throughout the interior of the country for many years. April 28th, 1839, the Armenian patriarch issued a new bull threatening terrible anathemas, in the name of the Father, Son and Holy Ghost, against all who should be found communicating with the missionaries or reading their books. Arrests and imprisonments were of constant occurrence. The native evangelicals were at their wits' end and the missionaries could see no way of deliverance.

Most fortunately for them, at that time the sultan was at war with Mohammed Ali of Egypt, and he called upon all the patriarchs to provide him with recruits for his broken army. The defeat of the sultan, his death, and the succession of his son, Abdul Medjid, with the loss of the Turkish fleet, threw all into consternation and made the most violent bigots forget for the moment to persecute. A fire in Pera which destroyed between three thousand and four thousand Armenian houses tended to produce a softening of heart against the persecuted.

While this condition of affairs prevailed at the capital the mission was pushing its advanced posts into the interior of the country where considerable numbers were found eager to procure copies of the Bible. Ecclesiastical warnings sent from Constantinople to the Armenians remote from the capital were given little heed. Violence had so subsided at Constantinople that the evangelical movement again began to accumulate momentum and force. A boarding-school for boys was opened in November, 1840, at Bebek upon the Bosporus, some five miles above Constantinople. This was under the superintendence of Cyrus Hamlin, against whom and his school all the fury of the papists and the Greek patriarch was directed, the Armenian patriarch refusing to join them. The demand for books increased. By 1841 it was

LEADERS, METHODS, AND ANATHEMAS

evident that a great reform movement was in progress which was destined to spread over the empire. Some of the leading persecutors were astute enough to see that an invisible but irresistible force was moving the Armenian nation. The spirit of reform swept over the country, awakening intellects, arousing consciences, and demanding intellectual freedom.

This continued for five or six years, during which time there was no separation of the "Evangelicals," as they were called, from the old Church. The missionaries always urged them to remain, exerting their influence not against the Church but against its abuses and superstitions. For the most part they attended public services in the old Church, and were recognized as members in good standing. The missionaries had no thought of changing these conditions, had they imagined it was in their power to do so. Hitherto the movement had been one towards reform within the Armenian Church and largely led by Armenians who were themselves loyal members. In persecuting, the Church was doing violence to its own.

In the beginning of 1846 the patriarch, alarmed at the extent as well as the power of the reform movement, inaugurated more coercive measures. On Sunday morning, January 25, at the close of the regular service in the Patriarchal Church, darkening the house and drawing a great veil in front of the main altar, a bull of excision was read against Priest Vartanes, an evangelical, and all of the followers of the "modern sectaries." Heaping every conceivable epithet of condemnation upon him he was expelled from the Church and forbidden as "a devil and the child of the devil to enter into the company of believers." All the faithful were forbidden to admit him into their dwellings or to receive his salutation or to look upon his face.

A wild spirit of fanaticism reigned. This most thorough and fanatical persecution began to search out the evangelicals, who were ordered to repair to the patriarchate and recant, or be forever cast out from society, from every social privilege, and from the Church. On the following Sabbath, with passions still more inflamed, a second anathema was read in all the churches, accompanied by the most violent denunciations by the patriarch, the bishop and the vartabeds. All of the evangelicals were pronounced " accursed, and excommunicated, and anathematized by God, and by all his saints, and by Matteos Patriarch." The patriarch not only cursed those who were readers of the Bible and believers in its teachings, but grave malediction was hurled against all who should harbor them or communicate with them. Printed copies of the last two anathemas were sent to every part of Turkey to be read in all the churches. Even to this point the evangelical Armenians had made no move to form a community separate from the old Church.

On the 21st of June, 1846, a day of solemn festival in the Church, the patriarch issued a new bull of excommunication and anathema against all who remained firm to their evangelical principles, decreeing that it should be publicly read at each annual return of this festival in all the Armenian churches throughout the Ottoman empire. By this act the Protestant or evangelical Armenians were completely cut off from any lot or part in the Gregorian Church. There was no hope of their being received back again except by their repudiating every principle of reform. This, of course, they could not do.

These excommunicated brethren immediately requested help from the missionaries. A meeting was held in Constantinople, made up of delegates from the different mission stations in Turkey, at which Dr. Pomeroy, later one of the secretaries of the American Board, was present. At that meeting, plans were drawn up for an organization among the evangelical Armenians of Constantinople. Consequently, on the first day of July, 1846, they came together and were organized into the First Evangelical Armenian Church. The church numbered forty members, of which thirty-seven were men. One week later an Armenian pastor, a former student in the school of Pashtimaljian, was ordained over the church. A pamphlet in Armenian was issued, containing their confession of faith and setting forth the reasons why, through the compulsory measures of the patriarch, they had been compelled to organize themselves into a separate body.

During the same summer, similar Armenian churches were formed in Nicomedia, Adabazar and Trebizond. The Mohammedans showed themselves sympathetic. A Moslem judge before whom some of the evangelicals had been haled, said, " We cannot interfere to protect you from excommunication, but so long as you abide by the declaration you have made we will protect you civilly. Your goods shall be as our goods; your houses as our houses; and your persons as our persons. Go in peace."

All subjects of the Turkish empire were registered as members of some recognized religious community. Each various Christian community like the Armenian, the Greek, and the Roman Catholic, had its recognized head at the Porte and through this head individual rights were protected. Every non-Moslem was compelled to claim his rights at the hand of his religious political head. If his claim were there denied, he had no redress. The Armenian patriarch was the recognized political superior of the Armenians. He had violently excluded all evangelicals from the Church and from all their inherited rights as Armenians. He no longer recognized such as members of his race, and not only refused to protect them and secure for them justice but he devised methods to direct a bitter persecution against them. These excommunicated "Protestants," as they were sometimes called, were the legal possessors of no rights or privileges in the empire that any one was bound to respect.

Conditions became intolerable, when through the intervention of the British legation the grand vizier issued in November, 1847, a firman recognizing the separate Protestant community with all the rights and privileges belonging to others in the empire, and declaring that "no interference whatever shall be permitted in their temporal and spiritual concerns on the part of the patriarch, monks, or priests of other sects." This firman protected the evangelical Greeks and Jews as well as the Armenians. As this charter was only ministerial in its scope and authority, in 1850 a new charter was granted the Protestants by Sultan Abdul Medjid, "completing and confirming their distinct organization as a civil community, etc."

This phase of mission work in Turkey has been dwelt upon at length in order to correct the impression which prevails in many quarters that the missionaries in Turkey aimed to divide the old Churches there and to separate out therefrom a body of Protestants. History makes it clear that every effort was made to prevent separation, and only after this had taken place, by the repeated and official action of the highest ecclesiastical authority, were any steps taken to organize a separate community, and even then this was done primarily to secure protection for the excommunicated Christians.

RESULTS

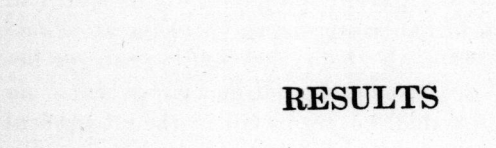

I HAVE had occasion to revert to the work of the accomplished and devoted band of American missionaries and teachers settled in these districts. In a thousand ways they are raising the standard of morality, of intelligence, of education, of material well-being, of industrial enterprise. Directly or indirectly every phase of their work is rapidly paving the way for American commerce. Special stress should be laid upon the remarkable work of the physicians, ordained or unordained, who are attached to the various stations. They form a steadily growing network, dotting the map of Asia Minor at Cæsarea, Marsovan, Sivas, Adana, Aintab, Mardin, Harpoot, Bitlis, and Van. At most of these points well-equipped hospitals are in active operation. From the very nature of their occupation they come more easily and rapidly into touch with the Turkish population and quickly gain their confidence.

Taking all in all, I regard the results following the foundation of this institution (Euphrates College) as among the most important and noteworthy secured by American effort in foreign lands. The whole work appeals most strongly to one whose chief duty is to aid and further the entrance of American wares in this land. I know of no import better adapted to secure the future commercial supremacy of the United States in this land of such wonderful potential possibilities than the introduction of American teachers, of American educational appliances and books of American methods and ideas. — PROF. THOMAS H. NORTON, Ph. D., United States Consul at Harpoot and Smyrna, Turkey.

XVI. RESULTS

WHILE these troublous scenes were being enacted, the missionaries were engaged in preparing and sending out evangelical Christian literature in the form of the Bible in the vernacular Armenian, Armeno-Turkish and Greek languages, and by fostering educational operations. As early as 1836 a school for Armenian girls was opened in Smyrna. A boarding-school for Armenian boys opened in Bebek in 1840 was so promising that in 1843–44 Secretary Anderson, upon a visit to Constantinople, recommended that this institution be strengthened. At that time it was decided to discontinue the special work to the Greeks and to open a high school for girls at the capital. The purpose of the seminary at Bebek was to train able and devout young men for the gospel ministry, that the newly organized churches might have proper leaders. In 1848 the seminary contained forty-seven students.

In 1847 some Christian literature found its way into Aintab in northern Syria. During that year and the next, missionary visits were made to the place. In 1849 Mr. Schneider took up his residence there, and Aintab became a regular mission station. In the midst of persecution the work spread with great rapidity. Preachers and colporters were forbidden by the Armenian primates to visit the neighboring towns, so evangelical tradesmen began a systematic visitation to outside places, plying their trade and preaching the gospel. The spirit of intelligent faith and religious liberty spread in all directions until the entire region was affected. In 1861 the church in Aintab had nearly three hundred members and the Sabbath congregation often numbered more than one thousand souls. The Sabbath-school then had nearly two thousand members. In 1855 Marash was occupied as a mission station, and these two places have since been the two central stations of that mission.

For nearly a generation after the separation of the Protestants took place there was more or less hostile feeling between the two bodies, although the number of the evangelicals rapidly increased. The spirit of inquiry was abroad among the Armenians and nothing could satisfy it but the truth. Travelers into the interior and visitors to Constantinople from the interior carried this spirit into the most remote sections of the country. The anathemas which had been communicated to the churches of the inland towns and cities had stirred up many questions and aroused alert minds to seek the cause. On the whole, the evangelical movement was most materially helped by these rude and bungling endeavors to suppress it by brute force. Wherever missionaries went they were met by a group of men, naturally among the most enlightened in all the community, who sought aid in the interpretation of the Scriptures, and who were eager to receive literature explaining evangelical truth.

Mission stations all over the country rapidly multiplied, and the number of Protestant churches increased. In 1860 forty Protestant churches had been organized, mostly among the Armenians, and twenty-two stations at which missionaries resided were in full operation. At nearly all of these stations, schools for boys and, in cases not a few, schools for girls, had been opened and these were well patronized. The printing-press was moved from Malta to Smyrna in 1833. The press always has been

RESULTS

and is still one of the most active and effectual agents for reform in the empire. During the first forty years of the work, from five to ten million pages of Christian literature were issued from the press each year, in five different languages.

In no part of the Turkish empire has the work of the missionary been more difficult than in Syria. Owing to papal supremacy there, which called to its service both Turkish and French political aid in its endeavor to thwart the missionaries and the evangelicals, no separate church of native Christians was organized until 1848 at Beirut, two years after the formation of the Evangelical Armenian Church at Constantinople. There was in that field no intellectually and morally dominant race to receive and extend the gospel as there was in Asia Minor and the greater part of the Turkish empire, while the races occupying Syria were for the most part hostile to each other and always mutually suspicious.

In 1858 direct work for the Bulgarians was begun by opening a station at Adrianople, which was followed by a station at Philippopolis and Eski-Zagra within the next two years. The Bulgarians were longing for political freedom and welcomed the missionaries with their new literature and education as calculated to strengthen them as a nation. For fourteen years the work among the Bulgarians was considered a part of the Armenian mission. In 1872 the European work was set off by itself as the European Turkey mission, which is almost exclusively for the Bulgarians. The condition of the old Bulgarian Church was similar to the Armenian Church, so far as need of reform was concerned.

The churches which were organized in 1846, among those cast out from the old Gregorian Church, were severely plain and simple in their form and ritual, as well as in their articles of faith. In the reaction from the rigid ritualism of the Church from which they had been driven, these evangelical Christians went to the other extreme, putting the emphasis of the service upon the sermon. Prevailing conditions demanded direct positive instruction in Christian living rather than new forms of worship. Had these people not been rudely excommunicated from the Church there is no doubt that they would have clung fondly to much if not all of the rich service of the old Church. Much place was also given to the reading of the Scriptures in the modern spoken language of the people and to congregational singing. The people were so eager for the sermon, and especially in the expository form, that large numbers who repudiated the name of evangelical, and who were among the persecutors of the Protestants began to demand that the priests of the old Church also expound the Scriptures. Few of them were able to accomplish this with any degree of success. Dr. Goodell published a volume of sermons in Armenian which were eagerly bought by the priests and preached by them to their people. Although the evangelicals had been violently thrust out of the Church, the spirit of reform in considerable measure remained.

During the first bitter years, when feelings were stirred up and controversy was rife, there was a wide breach between the Gregorian and Protestant Churches. After discussions all over the country, extending to nearly every village of importance, had settled the question that the modern version of the Bible in the vernacular was the unquestioned Word of God, there was actually no ground for continued separate existence. All Armenians accepted the modern Scriptures as the revelation of God to men

RESULTS

and an infallible guide to faith and practise. Neither did they have any scruples against the Bible being put into the hands of the people. Hence, as one might expect, the breach between the old and the new began gradually to heal. The spirit of bitterness, little by little, passed away until now it does not exist upon the old grounds which led to the separation.

In many places the Protestant pastors are now asked to speak in the old churches, and the children of both Gregorian and Protestant parents meet in the same Christian schools and upon exactly the same footing. In the theological seminaries of the missions there have been and now are students who are not Protestants and who are preparing for ordination as priests in the old Church. Many ecclesiastics of the Gregorian Church received the major part of their training for that service in the mission schools. During the last twenty years there has been little separation from the old Church. The missionaries have generally exerted their influence against it. Some Gregorians have tried to keep the controversy alive by claiming that the Protestants are not loyal to the race, but that charge has been so fully proven untrue that it is now little used.

In no instance have the missionaries for any length of time been the pastors of the native churches. At the first the policy was clearly settled that the only true and effective pastor of an Armenian church is an Armenian. The missionaries preach, and they have always been preachers, and some of them of great power, but this is quite different from being the settled pastor of a church. The rapid increase in the number of evangelical churches, each one of which demanded its own native pastor, compelled the missionaries to redouble their efforts to raise up and train an adequate number of worthy young men for these high offices. The seminary at Bebek produced men who have left the stamp of their piety, earnestness and ability upon the reform movement in Turkey. Some of these men came from the far interior of the country, and returning became the leaders in the new movement.

This seminary was ultimately moved to Marsovan, while other similar institutions sprang up at Marash and at Harpoot, in the eastern part of the country. A similar training-school became necessary also at Mardin, where the spoken language is Arabic, while in Beirut, Syria, a large training-school flourished. A whole educational system grew up out of the necessities of the work. This will be considered later when discussing the work of education in the empire.

The evangelical Churches were not denominational in any ordinary sense of that word. Their creed was the Bible in the language of the people and this was taken as the guide of their life. While the missionaries, because of their superior knowledge and experience in such matters, were constantly sought for advice, they did not exercise ecclesiastical control. These Churches were early advised to form themselves into Associations or *Unions*, as they were more generally called, for the purpose of mutual help. One such union was formed in the vicinity of Constantinople, and later one in Aintab and vicinity and at Harpoot and elsewhere. In these organizations missionaries could be only honorary members without a vote. They were composed of pastors and delegates from the churches, and held an annual meeting, with more frequent meetings of standing committees with varying functions. In some parts of the country these unions ordain to the gospel ministry and examine worthy candidates and grant them licenses to preach. It is not a Congregational system, neither is it Presbyterian, but it has worked well in developing native talent and directing it into right channels of action.

The development and strength in the evangelistic work in Turkey is due perhaps more to the leadership of a few individuals who seem to have been sent into the empire at a time most opportune. Dr. William Goodell, the first missionary of the Board to Constantinople, lived and labored there for forty-three years, or until 1865. With rare wisdom, patience and firmness did he direct the work through the period of fiery persecution and of organization of the Church and the Protestant community. Men are now there in the work, both missionaries and others, who were colaborers with him and who have helped to carry out the wise measures devised by him for the true reform of that people. Time would fail us to speak of Schneider, Dwight, Thompson and Riggs, of Post and the Blisses, of Wheeler, Farnsworth and a great multitude besides who gave their lives to build in the Turkish empire the pure, intelligent Church of Jesus Christ, to say nothing of the equally faithful and able company who are still there among perils and difficulties not less severe, but who know they are doing the Lord's work, and that they are in the place where he has called them.

At the present time the nearly two hundred evangelical Protestant churches in the empire, with some twenty thousand church-members, do not begin to tell the tale of what has been accomplished. The story is written in the awakened intellect of all classes and races, in new conceptions of what Christianity demands of its followers, and in a changed atmosphere affecting the life and character of nearly all the youth born in the last generation, and is destined to affect the empire still more vitally as the years go on. The seed of intelligent belief and of right living has been sown and it is finding soil in which to germinate. The fruit thereof shall be for the healing of the nation.

INTELLECTUAL RENAISSANCE

EDUCATION has accomplished more toward the regeneration of these lands than anything else. While it has been very broad, especially in the higher institutions, it has likewise been thoroughly permeated with Christianity. Though Robert College is not directly connected with any missionary society it "has exerted an incalculable influence for Christian life all over the empire. Among its graduates are many of the most prominent men in Bulgaria, and it is perhaps not too much to say that the nation really owes its existence to the influence exerted by President George Washburn and his associates. Its students have included representatives of twenty nationalities, and its Young Men's Christian Association is unique among the college associations of the world in that it is divided into four departments according to the prevailing language spoken, — English, Greek, Armenian and Bulgarian." The Syrian Protestant College at Beirut is likewise independent, though in closest sympathy and cooperation with the Presbyterian Board, North. Concerning the college, Mr. John R. Mott writes: "This is one of the three most important institutions in all Asia. In fact there is no college which has within one generation accomplished a greater work and which to-day has a larger opportunity. It has practically created the medical profession of the Levant. It has been the most influential factor of the East. It has been and is the center for genuine Christian and scientific literature in all that region. Fully one-fourth of the graduates of the collegiate department have entered Christian work either as preachers or as teachers in Christian schools." In less degree the same results noted in the case of these two institutions are furnished by the records of the American Board's colleges at Aintab, Harpoot, Samakov, Marsovan, and of its colleges for girls at Marash and Constantinople, as well as of the less ambitious Bishop Gobat School of the Church Missionary Society and the Beirut Female Seminary of the Presbyterians.— PROF. HARLAN P. BEACH, F.R.G.S. etc., in "Geography and Atlas of Protestant Missions."

XVII. INTELLECTUAL RENAISSANCE

IT has already been stated that in 1820 throughout the Turkish empire there was practically no modern education. The few schools which did exist were almost entirely ecclesiastical, maintained for the purpose of teaching a few men to conduct religious services. This was largely true of all schools, whether Armenian, Greek, or Turkish. Nowhere in the country were there schools for girls, the idea prevailing generally that girls could not learn to read, even if they were worth educating. The great mass of the people were unable either to read or to write. Ignorance even in the capital was dense, but it was much greater in the interior cities and towns. Often a large group of villages possessed not one person who could write or read a letter.

Argument is not required to show that no real reform could be introduced into the country without inaugurating some system of education. There must be produced readers and a literature if the intellectual and moral life of the people was to be raised. If the old Gregorian Church was to become enlightened in its belief and practise, there must be educated leaders as well as an intelligent laity. For this reason the missionaries began with an effort to awaken the intellects of the people. The Lancasterian schools that were so popular for a period in the capital had their value and exerted a good influence. The school of Pashtimaljian sprang from the aroused desire of the people for education and the conviction of the leaders of the Church that only educated leaders could be wisely trusted and followed. There were other schools supported and directed by the Armenians themselves, but springing largely from the persistent effort of the missionaries. Until 1839 it was hoped that all the work of modern education among the Armenians would be carried on by the Armenians themselves, so that the missionaries need not open schools of any kind.

As the zealous ecclesiastics became more and more suspicious, restrictive measures were applied. It was observed that those who studied in the schools were among the leaders seeking to reform the errors which were destroying the spiritual influence of the Church. It soon became evident to the missionaries that they must take a direct part in the work of education. In 1840 Bebek Seminary for training the young men was opened. The head of this school was Cyrus Hamlin, who the year before had arrived at Constantinople, designated to this work. He was a man of rare qualifications for the task assigned him, knowing no fear, never disheartened in the face of insuperable obstacles, of tireless industry, practical wisdom and unbounded resourcefulness and devotion to the cause to which he had given his life.

The seminary at Bebek was begun just as the persecution of the evangelicals at the capital was becoming acute. Early in his career Dr. Hamlin was impressed with the fact that the school must succeed in the face of direct opposition from Russia. During his first year in the mission, while he was learning the Armenian language, his teacher was suddenly seized at the order of the Russian ambassador and deported to Siberia. Dr. Hamlin and Dr. Schauffler repaired to the Russian embassy and protested against the high-handed proceeding. The ambassador haughtily replied, "My master, the emperor of Russia, will never allow Protestantism to set its foot in

INTELLECTUAL RENAISSANCE

Turkey." Dr. Schauffler, bowing low to the ambassador, gave the reply which has become historic, "Your excellency, the kingdom of Christ, who is my Master, will never ask the emperor of all the Russias where it may set its foot." From that day to this, the covert as well as open opposition of Russia to missionary work in Turkey and, most especially, to all educational work, has been unremittingly experienced. Consistently has Russia adhered to the policy thus outlined and the opposition from that source to-day is as bitter as at any other period.

Dr. Hamlin threw himself into the work of the seminary with all his intense and resourceful energy. Thwarted at a hundred points, he immediately changed his plans and appeared even to his persecutors to have gained the victory. For twenty years the work proceeded with emphasis upon industries when industrial persecutions were crushing the people, but always strenuous, and always supremely Christian and evangelical. He saw that a vernacular training was not sufficient for the full equipment of the young men under his care to prepare them for positions of largest leadership. The Jesuit schools taught their pupils French so that all their graduates knew a European language. As yet the Armenian literature was very circumscribed and most inadequate to meet the intellectual and spiritual requirements of intelligent directors of a great national reform movement.

This was the opinion of Dr. Hamlin, shared, as he felt, by the great mass of the Armenian people. But he was not fully sustained in it by his colleagues in the mission. The American Board, under the leadership of its secretary, Dr. Anderson, had declared as its policy that mission schools should not teach English or any other language than the vernacular to their pupils. To Dr.

Hamlin this seemed such a backward step that he resigned from the Board and began to work and plan for higher education among young men. The story of the building of the now famous Robert College under an imperial *irade* from the sultan, and upon the most commanding site along the entire length of the Bosporus, is now so well known that it need not be repeated.

The college became a reality and the scheme of education conceived by Dr. Hamlin and carried out in Robert College represented, within forty years of the time of his resignation from the Board, the fundamental policy of all the higher educational work in the empire carried on in both missionary and independent institutions. For nearly a generation, however, in mission schools little was done in European languages, and most of the education given was imparted through the spoken language of the people.

As early as 1836, four years before the seminary at Bebek was begun, a high school was opened in Beirut in which both Arabic and English were taught. This school was apparently a great success, but four years later the pupils, because of their practical knowledge of English, became so useful to the English officers, then quartered in Beirut on account of political troubles, that the school was broken up. No doubt this unfortunate experience had much influence in leading the Board to endeavor to exclude English from mission schools. In 1848, a seminary upon the purely vernacular basis was opened in Beirut with a view to training its students for useful service among their own people. This school was continued until the change in policy by the Board and the mission, when the English language again took its place in the curriculum.

ROBERT COLLEGE, CONSTANTINOPLE

SYRIAN PROTESTANT COLLEGE, BEIRUT, SYRIA

INTELLECTUAL RENAISSANCE

Whatever differences of opinion existed as to the place of English in the educational system of Turkey, there was practical unanimity in the belief that reform in the empire demanded the creation and maintenance of a system of schools which should include all grades, beginning with the primary. It was necessary to begin with the most rudimentary teaching before higher institutions could be sustained. The seminaries already referred to were not by any means colleges. They taught many studies of the lowest grades. As most of the pupils were mature in years, they made speedy progress and often astonished their teachers by their rapid advancement and clear grasp of abstruse subjects.

At every station where missionaries settled, schools sprang up and were at once widely patronized. In the large centers like Erzerum, Harpoot, Aintab and Marsovan, where the people were unusually intelligent and eager for an education, there was marked development and a rapid rise in the grade of the central schools. Colleges were not then developed, for there were no natives qualified to teach the studies of college grade, while there were no preparatory schools fitted to train students for college work. At that time the country itself was not in a condition to demand a college education. In the meantime Robert College was taking the lead in the higher education of men, although its work was then far inferior to the courses it now offers. Educators throughout the empire were closely watching the new institution upon the Bosporus, which became the pioneer and leader for the entire country.

When Dr. Hamlin was in the midst of his efforts to organize and construct a college for Turkey, the Rev. Crosby H. Wheeler, also from the state of Maine, was sent into Eastern Turkey as a missionary, and with designation to Harpoot. Dr. Wheeler, with energy similar to that of his fellow laborer, stopped upon his way at Constantinople and became acquainted with the educational work there developing. He took direct issue with Dr. Hamlin upon the subject of the value of English, but agreed with him upon the place of education in the work of reform. Some years later, when the educational work at Harpoot was well established, Dr. Wheeler felt so keenly upon this subject that he gave public notice in the seminary, of which he was the principal, that any student who was known to be studying English, even by himself or by the aid of one or two resident Armenians who had studied at Constantinople under Dr. Hamlin, would be summarily expelled from the school.

Dr. Wheeler, with his keen vision and unconquerable energy, while an evangelistic missionary of unusual power, became the pioneer of education at Harpoot. Under his leadership, strongly seconded by Rev. Dr. H. N. Barnum, the seminary for young men at that place rapidly developed until in 1878 it was merged into Armenia College, afterwards changed to Euphrates College. It did not require many years for Dr. Wheeler to see that no broad education could be given in Turkey without the use of the English language, so that he became one of the most energetic and enthusiastic supporters of an English education for all students in the higher institutions of learning in the country. The other high schools in the eastern part of Turkey became preparatory schools for the college, which was heartily endorsed by the people themselves, as appears from the wide patronage it received.

The same process of growth that has been noted at Harpoot took place also at Aintab, which is distant some

INTELLECTUAL RENAISSANCE

eight days' journey from Harpoot, upon the south side of the Taurus Mountains. In the meantime, the educational work at Beirut had made rapid strides, developing into a college which later became the largest and most influential educational institution in Syria and one of the most important in the Levant. This school early in its growth became detached from the mission Board and came under the control of a separate Board of Trustees in New York, and assumed the name of the Syrian Protestant College.

Space will not permit the mention in detail of Anatolia College at Marsovan, St. Paul's Institute at Tarsus, and the International College at Smyrna. The last two named are of comparatively recent elevation to the grade of college, while the former has had a record of college work of a quarter of a century. The school for the Bulgarians was established at Samakov, which is now in Bulgaria. It is called the Collegiate and Theological Institute, and is calculated to do for the young men of Bulgaria and Macedonia what these other institutions are doing for Asiatic Turkey.

The Syrian Protestant College at Beirut was begun as an institution of higher learning in 1866 by Rev. Daniel Bliss. What Dr. Hamlin was to Robert College and Dr. Wheeler to Euphrates College, and Dr. Tracy to Anatolia College, Dr. Bliss has been to this college in Syria. To-day with a campus of over forty acres, with five departments including medicine, pharmacy and a commercial course, and some seven hundred students in attendance from not less than fourteen nationalities, including Druses, Jews and Moslems, drawn from all parts of the Levant, from Persia and the Sudan, this college stands among the first in the empire for equipment and influence.

Educational work for girls started more slowly and

did not make such rapid progress as the work among young men. There was not at the beginning a manifest demand for the education of girls. Among all classes in the country was an inherent prejudice against the intellectual or social advancement of women. Intelligent men, not a few, were ready to argue that girls were incapable of learning to read, much less of acquiring a general education. It became necessary, therefore, to educate the men up to the idea that girls could learn and that it was worth while to educate them. In 1836 a school for girls was opened by the missionaries at Smyrna, then the most enlightened and advanced city in the empire. This passed out of the hands of the mission very quickly, being taken over with its forty pupils by the Armenian community. It was soon disbanded. In Constantinople, while no regular school had been opened for girls, a few of the most enlightened parents were providing instruction for their daughters by engaging as teacher for them one of the evangelical Armenians.

Under the impulse of the reform movement it was impossible to keep out schools for girls. These multiplied in the large cities first and then extended into the interior until they became almost as popular as the schools for young men. The Mission School for girls in Constantinople became the foremost institution of its kind in the empire. After passing through several changes, all in the line of progress, it became, nearly twenty years ago, the American College for Girls in Constantinople. It is to-day the most advanced school for the education of women in the Levant. Euphrates College at Harpoot has also a female department, while in Central Turkey at Marash there is now a collegiate school for young women as well as a similar institution at Smyrna. These schools, for both boys and girls, are overcrowded with students and have been from the beginning. It has been impossible to keep pace by enlargement with the increasing desire on the part of the people for the education of their children.

The collegiate institutions are well scattered over the length and breadth of the country. The two colleges for boys which are the nearest together are St. Paul's Institute at Tarsus and Central Turkey College at Aintab, and yet these are some four days' journey apart. The students in Beirut speak Arabic for the most part; those in Marash and Aintab use Turkish; those at Harpoot, Armenian; at Marsovan and Smyrna, Armenian, Greek and Turkish; and those at the American College for Girls and at Robert College, both in Constantinople, use about all the languages of the empire. English is taught in all, and constitutes, in some of the institutions, the only common tongue; as, for instance, in Robert College there are seldom less than a dozen nationalities and languages represented among the students. The only language they all wish to master is English. This becomes, then, the common linguistic meeting-place of scholars in the Ottoman empire.

All but three of the American colleges here mentioned are incorporated under the laws of either New York or Massachusetts, and so are distinctively and legally American institutions. All of them have some kind of official recognition from the Sublime Porte or from the sultan himself. Below the colleges are schools for both boys and girls of a grade which admits to the collegiate courses. This is true of schools remote from any college where the pupils who cannot go to a distant part of the country for an education are numerous.

Including the preparatory departments, there are not

less than six thousand pupils studying in connection with these collegiate institutions, and all under Christian training. The grade in many respects, if not in all, is equal to that of the ordinary American college. In languages they all give the broadest courses. In Euphrates College, for instance, there are from six to eight languages taught, at least six of which are compulsory. The courses of study are adapted to the needs of the country and with a view to training the students for the highest service to their own people. The college at Beirut has a medical department which is of great value to the country, drawing its students from every race.

When the direct collegiate work was entered upon, in every instance the theological schools were made separate departments or were entirely set apart by themselves. There are at the present time six distinct training-schools in Turkey which have for their object the preparation of young men for the gospel ministry. Two of these, namely the schools at Beirut, and at Mardin, in northern Mesopotamia, train their pupils for work among Arabic speaking peoples; the one at Harpoot, for work among the Armenians, where the Armenian language is chiefly used, although some of its pupils speak Turkish; the one at Marash for Turkish speaking peoples; the one at Marsovan for those who speak Armenian, Turkish and Greek; and the one at Samakov, Bulgaria, for Bulgarians alone. Attempts have been made to unite this theological work, but the long distance separating the schools and the time and cost of the journey to and from them, the barriers of the different languages, and the restrictions put upon all native students in travel, have made it impracticable to do so up to the present time.

In these institutions, by far the largest number of

INTELLECTUAL RENAISSANCE

teachers are natives of Turkey, some of whom, after taking a course of study in their own country, have had postgraduate work in Europe or the United States. In each case, the president is an American who is usually assisted by one or more Americans. It is the policy of all these institutions to employ as many thoroughly equipped native teachers and professors as can be secured consistent with maintaining the high intellectual and moral tone of the schools.

In no case are these free schools. The students are charged tuition, room rent, and board, and they also purchase their own books and supplies. Some of these colleges secure from fees and payments by the pupils nearly three-fourths of the entire cost of conducting the institution. This is true of Robert College at Constantinople and Antolia College at Marsovan, and others. In addition to the fees paid, the people of the country have contributed in some cases most liberally for the college plant. Aintab College is a marked instance of this. In recent years the early students who have prospered in business have given freely for the endowment of their Alma Mater, as in the case of Euphrates College at Harpoot. The willingness of the people to contribute for the support of these higher educational institutions demonstrates most unmistakably belief in their value.

Such numerous collegiate and theological institutions necessitate a large and ever increasing number of schools of lower grade all over the country. These have sprung up in nearly every village and are found in every town of size. They are for the most part entirely supported by the people themselves. The great value of the educational work done in Turkey by the missionaries does not lie alone in the schools of different grades now controlled and directed by them; it also appears in the thirst for education which manifests itself in independent village, parochial, and city schools, with more or less modern equipment, and stretching from Persia to the Bosporus, from the Black Sea to Arabia. There is much yet to be desired in this respect, but much has already been accomplished.

This educational work has made no perceptible impression upon the Jews, for whose special awakening mission work in Turkey was first undertaken. The Greeks have slowly responded and many young men from that race are found in Robert College at Constantinople, in the International College at Smyrna and in Anatolia College in Marsovan. The race as a race, however, in Turkey has not taken up the cause of modern education with vigor and pressed it with moral earnestness. It is the Armenian race that has responded most fully to the call of modern learning. By far the largest number of students of any one race in the schools in Turkey are Armenians. They constitute as large a proportion of the pupils of Robert College as that of any other race. While they number probably less than one-tenth of the inhabitants of the empire, they furnish a large proportion of its student body.

These modern educational institutions in Turkey are a mighty force in reshaping the life, thought, customs and practises of the people of that country. Men and women from these schools are taking leading positions there in the learned professions as well as in commerce and trade. Large numbers of former students in the mission schools are now prosperous merchants and business men in Europe and America. Through these men of modern ideas Western machinery and the products of our factories are finding their way into that part of the East in increasing quantities while the products of Turkey are in exchange

INTELLECTUAL RENAISSANCE

brought to us. It is probably true, as has been frequently stated, that the money given from America for the establishment and support of American colleges in Turkey is far more than returned, with large interest, in the form of increased trade with that country.

While the Turks have not largely attended any of the schools mentioned, nor have they seemed awake to the needs of a modern education, nevertheless, through the influence of so many advanced schools in the country they have been compelled to improve their own schools. It is an interesting fact that recently a far greater number of Mohammedan pupils are applying for admission to these schools. Few of the Turkish schools have as yet been thoroughly modernized; still, their entire educational system, if system it may be called, has felt the influence of the foreign schools. There have now and then been attempts at the organization of a Mohammedan college. These have for the most part proven egregious failures from the lack of preparatory schools to train students for the college and of teachers with proper training to carry on college work. They have also in cases, not a few, opened and conducted schools for girls, thus demonstrating their acceptance, in a measure at least, of the Christian doctrine of the equality of the sexes and the worth of womanhood. Many Moslem young men have been aroused to seek education in England or France.

THE PRINTING-PRESS

I CANNOT mention the American missionaries without a tribute to the admirable work they have done. They have been the only good influence that has worked from abroad upon the Turkish empire. They have shown great judgment and tact in their relations with the ancient churches of the land, Orthodox, Gregorian, Jacobite, Nestorian, and Catholic. They have lived cheerfully in the midst, not only of hardships, but latterly of serious dangers also. They have been the first to bring the light of education and learning into these dark places, and have rightly judged that it was far better to diffuse that light through their schools than to aim at a swollen roll of converts. From them alone, if we except the British consuls, has it been possible during the last thirty years to obtain trustworthy information regarding what passes in the interior. — HON. JAMES BRYCE, British Ambassador to the United States.

XVIII. THE PRINTING-PRESS

THE entire plan and purpose of missionary work in Turkey involved the printing-press. Only a little more than two years after the first missionaries to Turkey arrived upon the field, a press under the care of a missionary of the Board arrived at Malta, commissioned to print for the use of the Palestine and Turkish missions. At that time hostilities between Greece and Turkey were in progress and no port upon the Mediterranean was safe for the American press. Malta was under the English flag, and so proved for the time the best base for the literary operations of the mission.

Undoubtedly the earlier publications were too impracticable to meet the needs of the people of Turkey. The missionaries assumed ability in the untrained Oriental mind to grasp the thoughts of the West. In the list of what was printed at Malta during the first ten years are found such works as "Serious Thoughts on Eternity," "Guilt and Danger of Neglecting the Saviour," "Scott's Force of Truth," "Content and Discontent," "Inspiration of the Holy Scriptures." A great variety of books was prepared, for the most part, by those who knew practically nothing of the thought and life of the people who were supposed to read them.

In 1833 the political atmosphere had so cleared that the press was removed from Malta, the Arabic equipment going to Beirut in Syria, while the Greek, Turkish, and Armenian outfit was set up in Smyrna. During the ten years at Malta, over twenty-one million pages were printed in four different languages, namely modern Greek,

Italian, Armeno-Turkish, and Arabic. The largest amount by far was in Greek. No printing in Armenian was done until the press was set up in Smyrna and, previous to 1837, less than 175,000 pages had been printed in that language.

In 1829 it was decided to do more in the way of providing much needed books for elementary schools. One of these books was so popular that 27,000 copies were sold in Greece alone. In 1831 the Armeno-Turkish New Testament, translated by Dr. Goodell, was printed. That same year over five million pages of modern Greek were put out from the press. Nearly all of this was circulated about as rapidly as it could be run off.

The publication work in the Turkish missions outside Syria was carried on at Smyrna until 1853, or for about twenty years. The last and one of the most important works published there was the modern Armenian Bible translated by Dr. Elias Riggs. This one book has accomplished more to fix, unify, and simplify the modern spoken Armenian language than all other influences combined. What the King James version has done for the English speaking peoples, and Luther's Bible for the Germans, this scholarly and accurate translation has done for the Armenians all over the world.

Besides the Bible and strictly Biblical works, a large number of school-books of almost every grade as well as translations of choice parts of English literature were printed and sold. The eagerness of the Greeks and Armenians, and especially the latter, for a literature suited to their aroused intellectual condition made it possible to sell at cost much that was published. After the organization of the Evangelical Protestant Church, hymn-books in various languages were prepared and printed.

THE PRINTING-PRESS

It would be impossible in the limits of this discussion to give even a classified list of the publications issued from the mission presses of Turkey since printing began. The output upon the average from 1833, even to the present time, has been at the rate of from twelve to fifty million pages each year in not less than ten languages, including Bulgarian and Koordish. In some years this has been exceeded.

At Beirut in 1906 there were printed on the American press 152,500 volumes of distinctively Biblical literature, with a total of 47,278,000 pages. To this was added nearly 9,000,000 pages of other Christian and educational books, making a total of 56,000,000 pages of literature from this one press alone in a single year.

For the Bulgarians and the Armenians the missionaries practically created their new literature in the spoken tongue. Of the first one hundred books printed in the modern Bulgarian, some seventy were the product of the missionary press. The first grammar of the modern Armenian language was printed by the missionaries. The Koords had no literature of any kind, while their language is even yet unclassified. The New Testament was translated into that tongue, written with the Armenian characters, and in that language it was printed. Parts of the Bible have also been printed in the Albanian tongue.

The Bible has been translated into Arabo-Turkish, the language read by all the educated Moslems in Turkey north of Syria and is printed and widely circulated. This, with the Arabic and Syriac versions printed at Beirut, puts the Bible into the language of all the Moslems of Turkey, except the Koords and Albanians. As yet the former have only a part of the Bible, and the latter a very poor and fragmentary version, in their own language.

However great the influence of the press has been in the preparation of books and tracts, it has probably reached and permanently moved more people still by its periodical publications. Papers have been printed for more than a generation in Armenian, Greek, Armeno-Turkish, Greco-Turkish, Bulgarian, and Arabic which have had wide circulation among all classes, but especially among the evangelicals. These papers while religious, have also been newspapers, carrying into the remote hamlets of the interior information of the great outside world of which the masses were profoundly ignorant when mission work began. The influence of these papers can best be measured by the fact that when the cholera was approaching any section of the country, the missionaries were accustomed to publish detailed instructions regarding the best methods to prevent contracting the dread disease and what to do as soon as the symptoms appeared. Those who read the papers took great care to follow directions, and so the Protestants who usually knew how to read seldom suffered from the scourge.

When the cholera was raging with unusual virulence in Aintab, taking for the most part the Moslems and ignorant Gregorians and leaving the Protestants almost unscathed, a learned Moslem asked a missionary if God spread a tent over the Protestants that the cholera should pass them by. Through the periodicals in the various languages, the missionaries and leading Armenians have been able constantly to speak directly to the most intelligent classes of people in the entire empire.

When the missionaries began work in Turkey in 1820 there was no newspaper worthy the name in the country in any language and the number of books was but few. Printing was not left, however, entirely in the hands of

THE PRINTING-PRESS

the missionaries, for, after a time, to meet the demands of the different religious communities other presses were started. These were small in output and power and did not amount to much until within the last twenty-five years. During this time the Armenians have prepared and published some excellent text-books, many of which have been and still are in constant use in Protestant schools. They also have started a few periodicals that for the most part have little permanent value. The Moslems have done but little in the way of printing books or periodicals of any kind. They do not allow the Koran to be translated into the vernacular of the people, and it is their policy to exclude from their subjects, as far as possible, all knowledge of the outside world. The Moslem press has produced little of real value to the people.

Great freedom to the work of the press was given in the earlier days, all of which has changed during the last thirty years. While the Turks were never favorable to it, they tolerated it under a silent protest. Gradually the opposition became more and more open and violent. Undoubtedly all this originated among the Roman Catholics and the Jesuits, who even in the early days of the mission fought against the circulation of the Bible and Protestant books. They did much to stir up opposition to Protestant books, among the Greeks first and later among the Armenians, always assuming that the Bible is a Protestant book. There is no doubt that this hostility was helped on also by the representatives at the Porte from Russia. The Turks were not so much concerned with what they regarded as squabbles between the various Christian sects.

About 1878 Dr. Wheeler, President of Euphrates College, imported a printing-press into Harpoot, where he set it up and ran it with great industry for several years. Only a local work was done there, while the general publication operations of the missions were carried on at Beirut and Constantinople. In the eighties the Turkish government began to put severe restrictions upon the press. The one at Harpoot was silenced and has so remained to this day.[1] Strict rules were promulgated to restrict printing in the empire. Formal permission must be procured in order to own a printing outfit, and strict rules were formulated for its conduct. All matter to be printed must first be submitted to a royal censor whose stamp of approval upon every article is necessary before it is put upon the press. The same stamp of approval which carries with it the sanction of the sultan must be printed upon the first page of every book, otherwise its issue, circulation, or even possession by a subject of the empire constitutes a crime. This approval must be obtained for every edition of the same book. It is almost as difficult to secure permission to-day to print a new edition of the Bible as it was after the appointment of the first censorship to print the first edition. Permission to print a book like the Bible carries with it no authority to print separately any part of the same. These rules have greatly hampered the work of the press, but have not by any means been able to stop the constant output of useful books and periodicals in the leading languages of the country.

There is no department of missionary effort which has done more to open the eyes of the people and stir in them new desires and ambitions than this work of publication, taken in connection with the general educational operations. Many English books and periodicals find their way

[1] This press began operations again in September, 1908.

into these schools and are included in the libraries of the teachers and students. These too are subject to all the restrictive laws which hamper the press. The tendency is more and more to exclude all foreign books and periodicals and to have it almost a crime for a subject of Turkey to have in his possession a library of any kind. Many an Armenian has been arrested and thrown into prison for no other crime than the possession of a few harmless English books. No one has yet been bold enough to confiscate from the libraries of the missionaries the books which they possess, but this step has been repeatedly threatened. The officials, however, intercept many books in the mails or in transit by freight.

In all work of reform which marks the history of missions in that country this agency has been supremely potent. Undoubtedly to-day there is no more vitalizing force in the empire affecting the intellectual and religious life of the Moslems than that which is exerted not only through the Bible and especially prepared literature, but through books on science. These contain startling revelations to the old-school Moslem, since modern science runs counter to nearly every teaching of the Koran. He cannot deny their truth forever, and when he yields he has already met with a mighty intellectual and religious evolution.

MODERN MEDICINE

In the Turkish empire a remarkable impetus has been given to the material development of Asia Minor and Syria, which may be largely traced to the quickening influences of American missions. Mission converts are proverbially men of affairs, alert and progressive, and in full sympathy with modern ideals of progress. The change in their personal environment, and in the temper and spirit of their lives, testifies to new impulses, higher ambitions, and an enlarged and increasing sympathy with modern progress. As long ago as 1881, an incident of commercial significance was reported in The Missionary Herald. It was announced that through missionaries at Harpoot nearly five hundred sets of irons for fanning-mills had been ordered from the United States, native carpenters having been taught to make the necessary woodwork which would render them available. Since then the introduction of American agricultural machines has increased, in spite of the difficulties and heavy cost of transportation. The German government has interested itself in securing concessions for a railway through Asia Minor to Bagdad and Busrah, with the evident expectation that German trade will find in those regions a profitable field of exploitation. If it should prove true that Mesopotamia may become a source of supply for the grain which Europe needs, there is good reason to expect that American agricultural implements will find a new market in Asiatic Turkey. Owing to the large emigration of Armenians to the United States, and the long residence of American missionaries in Turkey, no foreign country is better known or more admiringly regarded by the entire Christian element of Armenia than the United States. Mr. Charles M. Dickinson, Consul-General of the United States at Constantinople, regards even the material returns of American mission work in Turkey as justifying in large measure the outlay. His opinion is expressed in the following paragraph:

"In all our efforts to extend American commerce, in the hard struggle to establish and maintain direct steam communication with New York, the opening of American expositions and agencies, and the introduction of new articles of manufacture, many of the missionaries have been willing pioneers, blazing the way for American exporters, and doing valuable introductory work through their knowledge of the local languages and their influence with the people. From every standpoint, therefore, I do not see how the American missions in Turkey, as they are at present conducted, can fail to be of distinct advantage to the commerce and influence of the United States." — JAMES S. DENNIS, in "Christian Missions and Social Progress."

XIX. MODERN MEDICINE

THERE was no purpose or plan at the beginning of missionary work in Turkey to make special use of the physician. Whenever a man was appointed as missionary who had taken a full course of medicine he was not sent out especially as a medical missionary, but went as did the others, with the understanding that he was an evangelistic missionary and was to use his medical skill as an auxiliary force. The outfit of the early medical missionaries, like Dr. Grant and Dr. Asa Dodge of Syria, was exceedingly circumscribed, consisting of a few standard remedies and simple instruments and appliances. There was no suggestion of a hospital or even a public dispensary. The medical missionary was able to transport the major part of his equipment upon a horse and apply his art at any point along the way. After the days of pioneering were passed and the various mission stations were well established, the medical missionaries began to prepare for a broader and more thorough work.

The country had no modern physicians when the Board began work there and no schools for medicine. The people submitted to the most loathsome and cruel methods of treatment at the hands of heartless old women and unskilled men who traded upon their sufferings. From the beginning the fullest confidence was placed in the American physician. He was deemed by the ignorant and needy masses as little less than a worker of miracles. His reputation gave not only himself but his missionary associates standing among all classes in the country. His presence often proved in times of stress to be a large element of safety for all members of the station. The Turkish officer and persecuting ecclesiast did not care to injure the man into whose hands their lives might soon be placed by disease or accident. They thought it good policy to keep on fairly good terms with the doctor.

Medical work in the empire took its earliest and strongest hold upon Beirut and Aintab. In the former place a hospital was erected and a medical school was in operation in the '70's. Aintab took the same step ten years later, but finally, for want of funds, gave up the medical school but continued the hospital. The next mission hospital to be erected was at Mardin. Until the last decade these constituted the main mission hospitals in the empire. Hospitals have followed at Cæsarea, Marsovan, and Van, while others are contemplated at Harpoot, Sivas, Erzerum, Adana, Constantinople, and elsewhere.

Many Greeks and Armenians have qualified themselves for medical practise in Turkey by taking a course of training either in the medical department of the Syrian Protestant College at Beirut or the medical schools in Europe or the United States. The laws of Turkey are so stringent in regard to the practise of medicine, or rather so oppressive, that it is almost impossible for a subject of Turkey to win great success in it. The law permits the arrest and imprisonment of a physician upon the complaint of any one that he did not correctly treat a case which ended fatally. When once he has been imprisoned it costs a round sum to secure release. This process repeated destroys practise and eats up profits. Many a well-trained Armenian doctor has been compelled to give up the effort and return to the United States. There are several Armenian physicians enjoying a good and honorable practise in this country. The foreign physician enjoys the extra territorial privileges of his country and,

MODERN MEDICINE

although often annoyed, is not seriously disturbed by restrictive measures. He practises under a license granted by an official medical board at Constantinople.

Medical missions in Turkey have opened the eyes of all classes to the value of scientific medical practise. Were it not for the restrictive measures of local officials, every town of considerable size in the country might now have its native physicians, the most of whom were trained in Christian schools. Until that time arrives the American missionary physician will have large place in the life of the country. His importance there is due to this fact, and also because of the confidence reposed in him by the higher Turkish officials. They regard the work of the medical missionary as supremely Christian. It commands their admiration. Not a little of the hold which the missionaries now have upon the country is due to his presence and work. In imitation of the missionaries, the Turks themselves have attempted, at different places, to maintain hospitals of their own for the care of soldiers and officers, but these have usually been of little value unless the physician in charge was a European or a man trained by the missions.

Medical work in Turkey is probably nearer self-support than that of any other missionary country except Japan. The people are willing so far as able to pay for medicines received and for services rendered. Wealthy officials often make a handsome present to the missionary physician treating them, thus making it possible to treat many poor without pay. The hospital at Mardin, for instance, receives in fees and in payment for medicines enough to meet all expenses except the salary of the American physician in charge. The hospital of Aintab receives little money from the Board.

Medical missions in Turkey are less hampered by officialism and hindered by opposition than any other form of missionary work. Physicians are more generally welcomed and their benefits more widely appreciated than anything else the missionaries do. While the other departments cannot be and ought not to be curtailed, much less abandoned, in view of all the conditions that prevail there with the constant scourges of pestilential diseases and the recurrence of violence and massacre in different parts of the country, there is an unlimited field for the operations of the Christian missionary physician who commends the gospel which he preaches to all with whom he comes in contact. At the same time, this work, compared with the extent of its influence, costs perhaps less than any other form of purely missionary service.

Missionary physicians, their medical schools, hospitals, dispensaries, and practise among the people have been a mighty force not only for alleviating suffering, but for breaking down the superstitions of all classes of people. The Arabs, the Koords, the Turks, as well as other Mohammedan races, have found their belief in *kismet*, or fate, greatly shaken by the practises of men who seemed successfully to set themselves against the will of God. They have seen the scourge of cholera stayed in its ravages by the application of modern scientific methods, and diseases which were regarded as almost universally fatal become little feared, and they are compelled to inquire if, after all, "whatever is, is ordained by Allah." Perhaps the medical work of the missionaries in Turkey has accomplished more in breaking down that benumbing belief in fatalism among the Mohammedans than all other phases of mission work together.

STANDING OF MISSIONARIES

My purpose is twofold: first to show the American people the kind of work in which the missionaries in Turkey are engaged, and second to assure them from personal observation that these missionaries do not encourage revolutionists or the revolutionary spirit. I am surer of nothing than I am of this. If you could see them at their somewhat thankless tasks you would regard them as the most consecrated men and women on the planet, as far removed from fostering rebellion as heaven is from earth, making the sacrifice of life and of all social and even domestic relations, and doing it with a cheerfulness which must command not only our respect but also our admiration.

The price to be paid for the enlightenment of the nation is very heavy, but these noble men and saintly women are willing to pay it, and I, for one, feel that my poor life amounts to nothing in comparison; so with a full heart, a heart with a big ache in it, I cry, "God bless them!"

The missionaries are the Sir Knights of modern times, their weapons are no longer swords, but ideas. They are to be found in all quarters of the globe, and they are always surrounded by ambushed perils. They are the representatives of a high civilization and of the best religious thought of the age, and are the little "leaven" which in good time is to "leaven the whole lump." I do not hesitate to say that they are doing more for the Turkey of to-day than all the European Powers combined. — GEORGE H. HEPWORTH in "Through Armenia on Horseback."

XX. STANDING OF MISSIONARIES

AT the beginning of work in Turkey all classes were suspicious of the missionaries. Experience with the representatives of the Roman Catholic and Greek Churches had led the Mohammedans and others to fear that their errand was not wholly religious. At the same time, it was impossible for one brought up in the atmosphere of Turkey not to confound religion with nationality. The American missionaries had one great advantage, for few even of the educated in Turkey ever heard of the United States. So there was not much alarm at the prospects of missionaries from the United States gaining political supremacy in Turkey. So far as the Turks understood, the country back of them was without strength or repute. This fact allayed the otherwise inevitable suspicion that they were political agents.

It required more than fifty years of residence in that country, accompanied by a life of constant devotion to the interests of the people, to remove the impression that the missionaries were there for what they could make out of it. The following conversation, which actually took place, illustrates fairly well the attitude of inquiry and doubt. The parties to it were a missionary and an intelligent Armenian in the interior of the country:

"You must receive a pretty large salary to lead you to leave your home and friends in America and endure here among us the hardships of this country."

"Quite the contrary," replied the missionary; "I receive what all American missionaries receive and no more, that is my bare living with no surplus."

"Then," the Armenian quickly replied, "you must expect, after you have learned the language, to receive some government appointment at a large salary."

The missionary answered, "Few missionaries have ever given up missionary work for a government appointment, and I have never seen one who would consider such an appointment, or who would remain in the country at all for diplomatic or consular service."

"There can be little doubt, then," said the questioner, "that in your country the missionary is held in high honor by all the people, so much so that it is worth all it costs to win it by a period of severe hardship in a land like this."

"You are wrong again, my friend," said the missionary, "for most of the people in the United States think a missionary is a fool to throw his life away in a strange and hostile land; and, besides, the missionaries enter upon the work for life; therefore they have no time left to go home and enjoy the honors that an admiring people might wish to thrust upon them."

"What are you out here for, anyway?" asked the discouraged guesser.

"We missionaries have come out here only to help the people of this country to establish worthy Christian institutions and to become better men and women."

"Surely there is some other reason," said the man as he walked away. "Who would ever bring upon himself such hardship and trouble for that?"

The true Christian motive that considers others' needs ahead of self-interest was little understood, and it required generations of missionary labors to bring the people to begin to understand it.

Times of great national distress like war, massacres,

famine, and plague, had given the missionaries unusual opportunity to prove to the people that they were there, not for their own personal comfort but to bind up the broken heart and give cheer to the downcast and the dying. Every added missionary grave, and they dot the country from Arabia to the Black Sea and from Persia to Salonica, was an added argument which no Oriental could answer, that the missionaries were there to minister and not to be ministered unto, and to give even their lives for others.

Through many vicissitudes and misunderstandings and misconceptions the missionaries have quietly continued their labors until, without doubt, it would be hard to find an intelligent man of any race or creed in the empire who does not believe them to be earnest, sincere, altruistic in their life and work. All classes have learned that in times of trouble the missionary is their best friend, no matter how much they may have abused him in times of prosperity. They know that he will always do what he believes to be for their best good, even though there may be a difference of judgment as to what is the best good.

In the midst of Oriental duplicity, the missionaries have established the reputation for speaking the truth. At first this was one of the severest puzzles to the Turks in the dealings of the missionaries with the government. They could conceive of no reason for telling the truth under such circumstances, so they were completely misled. The missionaries applied to the government, in an interior city, for permission to erect a schoolhouse. All school buildings were at that time opposed by the Turkish officials. The governor asked, "For what is the building to be used?" "A school," replied the missionary. "What are you going to keep in it?" asked the governor.

DAYBREAK IN TURKEY

"Scholars and teachers," was the reply. "Why do you want so large a building?" was the next question. "Because we are going to have many teachers and many pupils," said the missionary. "What are you going to manufacture there when it is done?" was asked. "Scholars," was the answer. The missionary was dismissed and for hours the council discussed the question. Not a man present believed that the proposed building was to be a school. They said, "Surely if he were building a school he would not have acknowledged it; it must indeed be something else." It was afterwards learned that they thought the building was to be an armory for manufacturing guns.

When Dr. Hepworth of the New York Herald took his famous journey through Armenia in 1896, he was given, by a Turkish governor, a letter of introduction to one of the American missionaries, Dr. H. N. Barnum at Harpoot, with the added statement, "He knows more about the conditions of the interior of Turkey than any living man, and you can depend absolutely upon what he says."

There is no class of people so trusted by the Armenians in Turkey, as well as by all other races, as are the American missionaries. Men who have been hostile to missionary work bring their daughters to the missionay boarding-school because, they say, "We know they will be safe here." All classes take the word of a missionary as absolutely true and without question. Money is put into their hands by the people for safe-keeping or for transmission to some other part of the country or out of it, without hesitation and without asking for a receipt.

There is no doubt that the Turkish officials, even though for reasons known to themselves they may oppose the erection of buildings for school or hospital purposes and hamper the missionaries in their general evangelistic work, have long since ceased to regard them in any other light than as men and women of unquestioned integrity and purity of life. Much testimony might be adduced to show the confidence that officials repose in individual missionaries. They may not like the higher educational institutions the missionaries have established there, which are leading an increasing percentage of the people to think for themselves, yet they do not now attempt to destroy them or their influence by making personal charges against the missionaries themselves.

Many Turkish officials of high rank have, in times of special stress, sought the counsel of missionaries, who had resided in the country many years, and who were generally reputed to have a wide knowledge of local affairs. It is interesting to note that in many instances the counsel obtained was acted upon, and later sincere gratitude was expressed.

After the Armenian massacre in 1895–96 the Armenian patriarch at Constantinople called the treasurer of the American Board at Constantinople and asked him to take complete charge of a considerable sum of money collected for relief. "For," said he, " I have no means of distributing this fund with assurance that it will, in any large part, reach the needy people, but I know that through the missionaries every dollar will go to the suffering poor."

The absolute integrity of the life and dealing of the missionaries with the people has done perhaps as much in that land of deceit and dishonesty to commend the simple gospel of Jesus Christ to all classes as any other single phase of the missionary work. It has come to be believed that a Christian of the missionary type must be true, honest, upright, and pure. This has great significance in a land like Turkey.

While Turkey has suffered but little from general famine or from plagues that have been sweeping in their character, still the missionaries have been compelled to devote much time and strength to the distribution of help to the starving and homeless, owing to oft-repeated political disasters amounting occasionally to open massacres. These began in 1822 at the time of the Greco-Turkish war when in Chios it was reported that fully fifty thousand lives were lost. The next great movement of the kind occurred in the Nestorian mountains when some ten thousand Armenians and Nestorians were said to have been put to death. In 1860 in the Lebanon and at Damascus about the same number of Maronites and Syrians were destroyed by the Turks and Druses. In 1876 occurred the well remembered Bulgarian massacres where some ten thousand Bulgarians were reported to have lost their lives. The last great and concerted movement of this kind occurred, as we all remember, in 1895–96, which extended from Persia to Constantinople and in which it is impossible to state with accuracy how many thousands of Armenians were massacred. The number has been placed at one hundred thousand, though this is undoubtedly too high.

In addition to these marked cases of violence and murder, the same process has gone on upon a much smaller scale for the last thirty years, causing terror, distress, and poverty, and calling for comfort and assistance. In the last three instances of general massacres reported above, the missionaries were upon the ground, facing no little of the peril and hardship with the people, and afterwards acted as agents for the distribution of relief to those who were left in abject destitution. Hundreds of thousands of dollars have passed through their hands for this purpose. With this money they have procured and distributed food and clothing to the starving and naked, while many lines of industry were opened to afford means of prolonged self-help.

The missionaries in Turkey have taken the lead in the application of principles by which, in the distribution of charity, much more can be accomplished, without impoverishing the recipients, by devising means whereby the aid received can be earned, at least in part. This same principle has been also carried out in the support of the large number of orphans saved from the massacres of 1895.

They have purchased and distributed seed for planting when famine conditions had exhausted the supply. In severer cases when their cattle had died or had been taken from them, missionaries have purchased oxen and loaned them to the farmers for putting in their crops. The policy of aid practised at all times has been to help the people to help themselves.

The missionaries in these and other lines of eleemosynary operations have demonstrated that they are the friends of all without reference to creed or religion. While these disasters have been terrible to contemplate and have brought immeasurable hardship and care upon the missionaries, they have yet opened new opportunities of approach to the people and have revealed the sincere desire to relieve them in their supreme distress. All classes have learned to trust the missionaries, and in times of trouble, all races appeal to them for assistance.

COMPLETED WORK

WHAT is in the future no man can tell, but the growth of pure religion in whatever form of church organization; the development of freedom of thought; the attainment of civil liberty, and that not merely for Armenia, but for Greek, Nestorian, Jacobite, and even for the Turk himself, depends upon the continuance of the influences for a higher life that have been at work during the past sixty years, and that depends upon the missionaries being supported at their posts. Theirs is no sectarian work. They stand as the friends of Gregorian Armenians, Roman Catholic Chaldeans, Nestorians and Jacobites as well as of those in closer affiliation with the Protestant Churches of Europe and America. America should stand by them and demand their full protection. It is our right by treaty; it is our right by the duty we owe humanity, by the duty we owe to our tradition as a liberty-loving nation. We have no political ends to serve; we want not a square foot of the sultan's domains; but we stand, as we have always stood, for freedom for the oppressed, for the right of every man to worship his God in the light of his own conscience. — EDWIN MUNSELL BLISS, in "Turkey and the Armenian Atrocities."

XXI. COMPLETED WORK

IN order to understand the methods employed in planting missions in Turkey and the permanent results following, one must have a clear idea of what the missionaries were attempting to accomplish. Perhaps we make the subject clearer by stating first some of the things they were not attempting to do.

They were not attempting to plant American churches in Turkey over which the missionaries should preside as pastors and which should be under the control and direction of the mission.

They were not attempting to transport into Turkey American churches, and American schools, and American customs and dress or anything else that is American.

They were not attempting to plant churches or schools or any other line of Christian work which should be perpetually dependent upon contributions from America for their maintenance.

What then, to speak positively, were some of the things the missionaries were attempting to do in Turkey? It should be stated at the outset that no settled policy was clearly in the mind of any one missionary at the beginning of the work. When missionary work began in Turkey no one, not even the officers of the Mission Board, had framed such a policy in detail. All had one vague desire and purpose, namely to preach the gospel of Christ to the people who dwell in the Turkish empire. At first, as has been stated, there was no intention of organizing churches separate from those already in existence there. It was expected that the missionaries upon the ground would shape and adopt their measures as necessity demanded. Men of broad culture, deep piety, and sound common sense were appointed to the fields, and to them was entrusted the responsibility of evolving a policy for themselves.

When independent Protestant churches were organized in 1846 it seemed the only natural step to ordain over them pastors from among their own people. There were several able and well-educated Armenians whose fitness for this office was unquestionable. At any rate, there were not enough missionaries upon the ground to fill these positions. Perhaps this last fact helped materially in settling the policy of a native pastor for a native church. Be this as it may, there was a speedy recognition of the right of the native church to have a pastor of its own from among its own race. This was early recognized as good policy, and was put into operation.

It does not, however, seem to have occurred to the missionaries then that the native churches had the same right to support the pastor thus ordained over them. The missionaries were there to see that the Christian work was carried on, and, to their minds, a most important part of it was to provide for the expense of the churches they had been agents in forming. In the annual reports of that period we find no allusion to payments by the people themselves for the support of their pastors. That was regarded as a part of the service missionaries were to render, and the people seemed perfectly willing to have it so.

In 1856 Crosby H. Wheeler was sent out as a missionary and in 1857 he was assigned to Harpoot in Eastern Turkey. He had received a thoroughly practical training in business and as a pastor in Maine before going out. While profoundly earnest in his purpose to Christianize the people of Turkey, he had little sentiment in his make-

A CLASS OF NATIVE STUDENTS, GRADUATES FROM THE AMERICAN COLLEGE FOR GIRLS, CONSTANTINOPLE

up and was eminently practical in all he undertook. He soon discovered that the churches in Turkey were regarded by the people as belonging to the missionaries, since the missionaries paid all the bills. Many who attended felt it to be a favor they were conferring upon the missionaries. A church in the city of Arabkir, some two days' journey northwest of Harpoot, was in need of a stove. Dr. Wheeler ordered one from America, paid the bill, even for transportation to Arabkir. One of the deacons of the church received the stove and set it up, and then sent a bill for his services to Dr. Wheeler. This turned the tide. Dr. Wheeler from that time became the champion of self-support for native churches, as a fundamental principle of self-government and self-propagation.

The people, for the most part, did not welcome the change. They were Orientals, and could not see why the American Christians should not have the privilege of supporting their pastors and meeting all the cost of their churches if they so desired. Dr. Wheeler, by pen and voice, advocated the policy with great energy and force. The wisdom of it was recognized by the officers of the Board. It gained general approval from most of the missionaries in Turkey, but many of them hardly dared to apply it vigorously in their own immediate community. It required no little courage to adopt and put through so unpopular a measure. The principle was a right one and could not but prevail. The wiser Armenians and Greeks saw that only in this way could they secure for themselves liberty and independence of action befitting their ability. While their desire for money inclined them to cling to the old custom, their love of freedom forced them towards self-support.

The same principle was applied to the missionary

schools. At first they also were free, but in the Orient no real value attaches to that which costs nothing. Schools that are free can be attended or not as the pupil sees fit. Books given away are easily lost or destroyed and are never valued. To command respect for the schools and insure regularity of attendance it became necessary to charge the pupils tuition. A pupil for whom tuition had been paid could be depended upon to be present when not seriously sick. Books and slates when purchased were cared for and used. Dr. Wheeler once spent several hours in persuading a man to purchase a two cent slate for his boy in school. The contest was for the principle, not the two cents. It is needless to say that Dr. Wheeler carried his point.

This principle is now a well-established policy throughout the Turkish missions. Native churches, as soon as they become financially able, assume the entire expense for themselves. No missionary is the pastor of a native church. The weaker churches pay what they can, the missionaries supplementing with the understanding that the mission's aid shall diminish as their financial strength increases.

Many Protestant schools in Turkey to-day receive no aid from mission funds. The people assume that an education has a real value for which they are willing to pay. Some of the colleges receive in tuition fees as much as three-fourths of the cost of conducting the institution. With others differently situated the proportion is less but all get no small part of their income from the students. Probably the higher educational institutions in Turkey secure as large if not a larger part of their running expenses from the pupils than do similar institutions in any other country in the world.

The same principle applies also to literature and to

COMPLETED WORK

medical treatment. The people pay liberally for all the products of the press, whether it be in the form of periodicals or books and tracts. Missionary physicians early learned that they could accomplish more good by charging fees for service and for medicine in all cases where the patient is able to pay. The patient who receives medicine free when he has money to pay for it is apt to defy all directions, or even not take it at all unless he likes it. Medicine that has been paid for is pretty sure to be taken. Some of the hospitals in Turkey, apart from the salary of the missionary physician in charge, are practically self-supporting, the fees of the patients and the sums paid for medicine being sufficient to meet the cost of attendants, supplies, and the care of the hospital.

The deserving poor, however, are not turned away. In schools methods of self-help are provided for students who have no funds with which to pay tuition, so that their self-respect and independence are not destroyed. In the same way provision is made for books. In cases of sickness, no one who is worthy is ever refused treatment by the missionary physician because he has no money to pay.

This principle of self-support has become a fixed part of the work in Turkey. The people are now thoroughly committed to it. They recognize that the mission is not there to transplant institutions from abroad, but to sow seed from which institutions may grow in the soil of Turkey, watered by Turkish showers, warmed by the Turkish sun, cultivated and cared for by Turkish hands. Much greater progress would have been made in self-support had it not been for many overwhelming disasters which have swept over the empire at intervals since missionary work began there. First it was devastating wars with Greece, with Egypt, and with Russia. Then came famine and massacre, the latter paralyzing trade, killing the wage-earners, and driving many of the most enterprising from the country. Had the Greeks and Armenians in Turkey been free from these terrible disasters for the last generation, it is safe to say every missionary church, school, hospital, and press would be to-day entirely independent of financial aid from this country. There would probably be need of missionaries for some time to come, and money from this country might still be called for to open new sections of the country, as, for instance, in Koordistan, and Albania, and Arabia, but in the old fields ample financial support would easily be supplied by the people themselves. In 1907 in spite of their poverty and distress the people connected with the American Board missions alone paid for their own churches, schools, and missionary medical attendance over $128,000, — a sum far in excess of what was paid by the Board to support the same work. We may confidently expect that if a new imperial policy should be put into operation and Turkey afford safety to life and property and liberty of conscience and judgment to all her subjects, there would be a marked advance in the support of all Christian and educational work in the country, and a rapid enlargement of all such institutions.

Much has also been accomplished in the line of self-propagation and aggressive Christian work. Various organizations of native Christian leaders, like the Bithynia Union of Western Turkey, organized in 1864, the Harpoot Evangelical Union organized in 1865, the Cilicia Union of Central Turkey, and similar organizations in Marsovan and in Bulgaria, as well as in other places, have rendered loyal service in the work of evangelization. These Unions have cooperated with the missionaries in aggressive operations as well as in the direction and supervision of the churches already organized. Their annual meetings have been marked events in the history of the churches. In these the missionaries are only honorary members, the native brethren taking the burden of responsibility. In some of the Unions, as at Harpoot in Eastern Turkey, a committee is annually appointed to cooperate during the year with the missionaries in looking after and directing work in the churches and schools as well as in planning and executing general evangelistic movements.

What the native churches are doing in the line of expansion is best exhibited in the Koordistan Missionary Society which had its beginning nearly forty years ago in the Harpoot Evangelical Union. This society was formed for the purpose of carrying the gospel and the advantages of a Christian education to the Koordish speaking Armenians who dwelt in the heart of Koordistan between the Harpoot, Mardin, and Bitlis stations of the Board. Funds were collected, visitations made, and promising Koordish speaking students from that country were brought to Harpoot and educated at the expense of that society and later returned to their people as teachers and preachers. As the work enlarged, evangelical churches in other parts of the country joined in the enterprise until it has come to be recognized as a work belonging to evangelical Armenians wherever found. Many Armenians in the United States have liberally contributed to sustain this society. The Armenians give freely for any Christian work that appeals to their national pride or that takes hold upon their sympathies.

In more recent times the alumni and students of Euphrates College who have gone to England or come to this country have contributed for providing scholarships in that institution for the education of poor but deserving students. While some are endowing scholarships, others propose to provide permanent professorships in the college. All this is additional evidence that, the Armenians once assured of safety to life and property, the Christian educational work in Turkey will speedily become largely, if not entirely, self-supporting. The Greeks, among whom much less work is carried on, would not fall behind in self-support.

INDUSTRIAL AND RELIGIOUS CHANGES

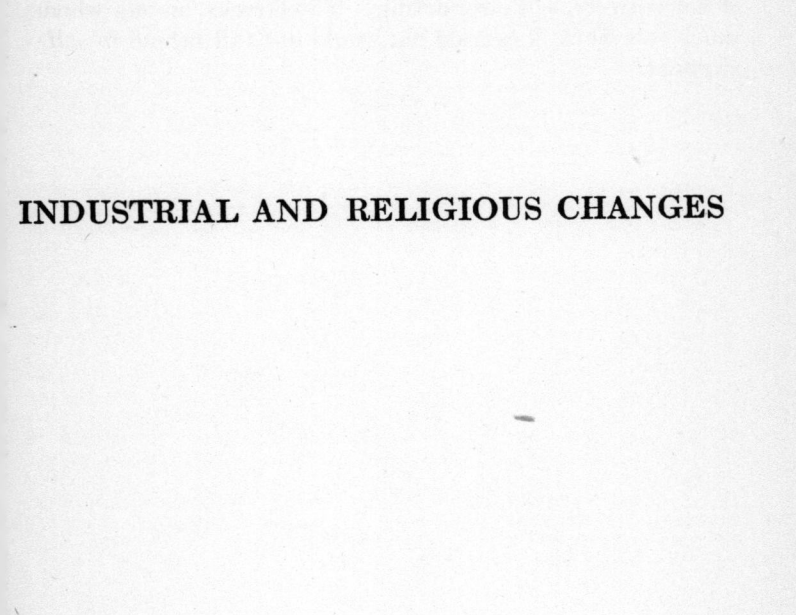

In the year 1860, in a public address in the city of London, the Earl of Shaftesbury paid the following tribute to the character of the American missionaries in Turkey: —

"I do not believe that in the whole history of missions; I do not believe that in the history of diplomacy, or in the history of any negotiations carried on between man and man, we can find anything to equal the wisdom, the soundness, and the pure evangelical truth of the body of men who constitute the American mission. I have said it twenty times before, and I will say it again — for the expression appropriately conveys my meaning — that 'they are a marvelous combination of common sense and piety.' Every man who comes in contact with these missionaries speaks in praise of them. Persons in authority, and persons in subjection, all speak in their favor; travelers speak well of them; and I know of no man who has ever been able to bring against that body a single valid objection. There they stand, tested by years, tried by their works, and exemplified by their fruits; and I believe it will be found that these American missionaries have done more toward upholding the truth and spreading the gospel of Christ in the East, than any other body of men in this or in any other age."

Mr. William T. Stead once said, "How many American citizens, I wonder, are aware that from the slopes of Mount Ararat all the way to the shores of the Blue Ægean Sea, American missionaries have scattered broadcast over all the distressful land the seed of American principles. When General Mosseloff, the director of foreign faiths within the Russian empire, visited Etchmiadzin the Armenian patriarch spread before him the map of Asia Minor, which was marked all over with American colleges, American churches, American schools, American missions. They (the American missionaries) are busy everywhere, teaching, preaching, begetting new life in these Asiatic races." — From "Memoirs of William Goodell."

XXII. INDUSTRIAL AND RELIGIOUS CHANGES

INDUSTRIALLY Turkey was ages behind even at the beginning of the last century. Practically nothing modern had entered the country from without and found acceptance there. The agricultural implements in use were of the same primitive character as those of two thousand or more years before. The plow of Abraham's day, made of the branch of a tree and only scratching the surface of the soil, was the only plow known, and it is not by any means extinct. The winds of the plains winnowed the grain, and the old threshing instruments with teeth still performed its ancient service upon the threshing-floors of earth.

In some respects the people were more jealous to guard their methods of work than they were their beliefs. It was found, however, that when a man had enlarged the horizon of his thinking, he was far more susceptible to suggestions as to his method of living and working.

Little by little new tools were brought in and made use of by native carpenters. Winnowing-mills for cleaning up threshing-floors, after years of opposition, won favor and are now found everywhere. In some sections cotton-gins run by water-power have brought a blessing to the farmers, while now and then a modern plow and other improved implements are finding acceptance. The sewing-machine is found in almost every town of importance, and the kerosene lamp has completely changed the character of multitudes of homes and greatly multiplied the possibilities of intellectual improvement and social reform.

The first electric telegraph instrument ever set up and operated in the empire was exhibited to the sultan of Turkey by Cyrus Hamlin, the missionary. The potato, the tomato, and other vegetables have been introduced into various sections, and in many cases have become regular articles of diet and staples in the market. Space forbids mention of the many industrial, mechanical, and economic improvements which have entered the country through the influence and even by the direct exertions of the missionaries.

All this in the earlier years was incidental to the mission work. During the last twenty years deliberate plans to teach industries have been made by the missionaries in some of the leading schools. While this industrial instruction was begun for the purpose of affording an opportunity to worthy but needy students to earn their way through school, the experiment proved that there was still another advantage not second to this in importance, and that was the educational value of practising an industry, as well as an economic value to the student and to the country. Industrial plants have been attached to some of the higher educational institutions like Anatolia College at Marsovan, where the results have amply justified the effort. It is surprising to see how rapidly new industrial ideas are disseminated from such a school.

At the time of the massacres of 1895–96 a large number of orphan children, both boys and girls, were taken in charge by the missionaries. These numbered many thousands. Their presence and needs forced the adoption of methods by which they could earn a part, at least, of their own support. Various industries sprang up wherever orphans and widows were found gathered into homes superintended by the missionary. These activities include cabinet

INDUSTRIAL AND RELIGIOUS CHANGES

work, carpentry, tinsmithing, blacksmithing, baking, embroidery, lace-making, with many other trades, besides silk culture and farming. As the children are bright and quick to learn the use of tools and remarkably good at imitation, marked progress is made. It is inevitable that out of these industrial plants will come new ideas and new industrial and mechanical impulses. Many of the young men who have come to the United States have learned trades which they will carry back to their own country as soon as they are satisfied that liberty is given them to return in safety. Probably industrial reform has not taken hold of the country as yet with the same force as other reforms. One prominent reason for this is that all industries are discouraged by the government. We can expect but moderate results until there is a change in this respect in the policy of administration.

Many changes in the construction of houses have taken place in the interior of the country. Wooden floors are rapidly coming into use, and windows admitting light and often with a few panes of glass are found even in remote villages. The one-story buildings in agricultural villages in which the family and the cattle during the winter occupied one room, are having a second story added for the family with pure air and with plenty of light. This one change alone is of inestimable value in lifting up and improving a people. Whitewash made with lime is freely used upon the inside of the living rooms and much pride is exhibited in the surroundings of the home. All this indicates a decided advance in family life and in the desire for what is civilized and wholesome. Every step forward is permanent. The industrial advance goes hand in hand with the introduction of comforts in the home. The possibilities for rapid enlargement of these reform measures are innumerable as soon as freedom of action and safety to life and property are assured.

Enlightened by education, chafing under the restrictions which crushed all enterprise in that country, and knowing about the large freedom and the wider opportunities open to all in the United States, a large number of Armenians have left their homes in Turkey for this country. Emigration began largely from Harpoot, but has extended now to all parts of the country, until it is estimated that there are now in the United States more than thirty thousand Armenians, with perhaps as many Greeks, Bulgarians, Albanians, Turks and Syrians. Many of these have become prosperous business men, worthy and loyal citizens of the United States. Others are farmers, professional men, and laborers in factories. Some have returned, but the Turkish government is suspicious of all, and especially of Armenians who have been in this country, and is likely to deport them if they succeed in passing the guards at the frontier. In proportion to their numbers, the Protestants in Turkey have furnished by far the largest number of emigrants. They were the first to come into closest contact with the American missionaries and to catch the spirit of modern education. It was most natural that they should be the first to turn their attention to this country as the land of the greatest opportunity. Many have come here to secure more education for work among their own people at home, but the severity of Turkish rule has hitherto kept the most of these here. Many Armenian Protestant churches and congregations have been formed in this country, at points from Boston to California, and in every case the pastors and preachers were trained at mission schools in Turkey. If it prove true that old restrictions are removed and safety and freedom assured to these exiles

INDUSTRIAL AND RELIGIOUS CHANGES

from their fatherland, no doubt the greater part of these will return with joy, carrying back with them not only the capital they have secured, but the enterprise and skill they have acquired in their experience here. Many of these men may soon become a great force in aggressive commercial Christian and educational enterprises for their own people.

The missionaries set out to aid the Armenians and other races in Turkey to an intelligent and reasonable faith and practise. Separation from among the Armenians was forced upon the evangelicals, as we have already seen, but the line that divided the Protestants from the old Gregorian Church did not mark a cleavage between those who seriously thought upon religious matters and those who were blind followers of the Church. Many thoughtful men remained in the old Church, and the discussions that produced so much disturbance outside were carried on in greater quietness, even among the clergy. There were two reform movements proceeding at the same time; one through the propagandism of the Protestant or evangelical body, separated in 1846 from the old Church by the action of the Church itself, and the other a much less marked but no less sincere spirit of investigation and inquiry continuing within the old Church. The general reform movement had been too rapid and aggressive for the conservative elements of the Church, but after the withdrawal of the most active leaders the reform spirit continued to develop and exert its influence.

These two widely divergent parties of sixty years ago have now drawn toward each other. There are probably to-day more intelligent evangelical believers within the old Gregorian, Greek and Syrian Churches than comprise the entire Protestant body. Separation no longer takes place in any marked degree. The same men preach occasionally in both Protestant and Gregorian churches. Evangelical teachers are engaged without dissent to teach Gregorian schools, while in many instances there are more Gregorian than Protestant pupils in Protestant schools.

Gregorian young men preparing themselves for orders in their Church are welcomed to the Protestant theological schools where they stand upon precisely the same footing as the Protestant youth with that ministry in view, while missionaries are invited to give lessons in Gregorian theological schools.

The Gregorian Church, as a whole, while yet far from the goal reached by many of its strongest supporters, is making advance towards an intelligent faith and practise. No longer do the leaders believe that there is virtue in the forms of worship or salvation in submission to the demands of the priesthood. They believe that true religion consists in true belief and right living and to this end they strive.

It is also evident that the Mohammedans have been perceptibly affected by reading the New Testament; thousands of copies have been sold them. Whereas heretofore they had interpreted Christianity by the lives of the people among them who bore that name, they are now studying the sources and see that between the two there is a wide gulf. They have been compelled, in self-defense, to search their own religion for fundamental truths of high character in order to prove to the reformed Christians that Islam is not as bad as it appears in the lives of many of its adherents.

In a word, all classes in the empire are learning that religion is a matter of conviction and life, and not of form, and that it manifests its true character in the acts of its followers, and not in the boasted declarations of its leaders.

AMERICAN RIGHTS

It has been stated by American officials in 1895 and 1896 that the missionaries, having forced themselves into Turkey against the will of the government, had no legal rights there and no claim to protection. The officials who made these statements must have been wilfully ignoring the facts of recent history. The missionaries were supported and encouraged by the three sultans, Mahmud the strong, Abd-ul-Medjid the weak, and Abd-ul-Aziz the weaker. They stand on a firm basis of treaties, special enactments, and concessions, — a basis in which the present sultan, with all his acuteness and his hatred of mission work, could find no flaw. Had it been possible to argue with a shadow of plausibility that the mission was against the law, or that it was not guaranteed by enactments inviolable even by a sultan protected by the six Powers, the property would have been destroyed and the mission silenced. The attempt was made, but failed; and the action of officials who destroyed mission property at Kharput, etc., was ostensibly disowned.

Further, the action of strong, free American life in Turkey must always tend to strengthen the movement there towards that freer and more elastic order which belongs to all the English-speaking peoples. But, though the mission work has, undoubtedly, exerted a great influence on the political situation in Turkey, the mission policy has studiously and consistently been non-political, and has zealously inculcated the doctrine of non-resistance and obedience to the existing government. — PROF. W. M. RAMSAY, D. C. L. in Preface of "Impressions of Turkey."

XXIII. AMERICAN RIGHTS

THE right to exercise their functions as a class possessing special privileges had been granted to ecclesiastics of Christian nations by the voluntary extension of the Edict of Toleration of 1453 given by the Ottoman government after the fall of Constantinople. Turkish usage for nearly four hundred years was the warrant for the entrance of American missionaries into the country and their assurance of immunity from official molestation.

They entered without diplomatic negotiations between the United States and Turkey. Not, indeed, till ten years after American missionaries had begun work in Turkey was the first treaty between the United States and that country concluded. Previous to that time the missionaries were protected by England, which had treaties with the Ottoman government conceding extra-territorial rights to all British subjects. The Sublime Porte did not seem to recognize any difference between an English subject and an American citizen for all were "Frank Christians" to him, hence the protection afforded was ample.

It cannot be predicted as in the case of most countries how many and what ordinary international rights will be conceded to foreigners by the Ottoman government. Rights in Turkey are based not upon any principle of international law usually prevailing between Christian nations but upon special treaties which bear the name of "Capitulations" and "Concessions." Intercourse of the Christian world with Mohammedan countries does not proceed according to the law of nations. International law as practised by the civilized nations of Christendom is an outgrowth from the communion of ideas existing between them and rests upon a common conception of justice and right. Between the Mohammedans and the Christian nations of Europe and America there exists no such common idea or principle from which could result a true international law. Relations one with the other have, therefore, to be regulated by special "capitulation" or "concession" granted by the ruler of the Mohammedan country.

For this reason, even to the present time, the law of nations as known and practised throughout Christendom has not been applied in the relations existing between Turkey and the Christian Powers. But ever since the Sublime Porte, under stress of circumstances, began to abandon most reluctantly and by slow degrees its ancient usages towards other nations, and imperfectly to adopt those of Christendom, its rule of international conduct has gradually approached that of Europe.

A capitulation on the part of the Turkish empire is regarded by the sultan and his associates as a concession to foreigners, which they have a right at any time to annul or destroy if, in their judgment, such annulment or destruction is for their advantage. The sultan does not wish to consider a capitulation as imposing a perpetual obligation upon him or his officials. It is a privilege rendered foreign powers which can be withdrawn without notice and without explanation. Only in view of these facts can the treatment of missionaries and other foreigners by the officials of Turkey be understood.

The Porte has agreed at various times to exercise no preference towards any of the states with which it has treaties, but to make them all share alike in the benefits

AMERICAN RIGHTS

of the provisions contained in the treaties it has entered into with each. In all its treaties of commerce since 1861, the expressed statement is, " That all the rights, privileges, or immunities which the Sublime Porte now grants or may hereafter grant to the subjects, vessels, commerce, or navigation of any other foreign power, the enjoyment of which it shall tolerate, shall be likewise accorded and the exercise of the enjoyment of the same shall be allowed, to the subjects, ships, commerce, and navigation of the other powers." It is evident from this quotation that every nation holding treaty with Turkey has equal rights and privileges with those of any nation treating with the Ottoman government.

Without dwelling at length upon the various treaties and the steps which led to their formation, it will suffice to say that these include, among many other things, the following privileges:

Permission to foreigners who come upon Moslem territory freely to navigate the waters and enter the ports of the same, whether for devotion and pilgrimage to the holy places, or for trading in the exportation and importation of every kind of unprohibited goods. Exception is made, however, with reference to the Hejaz Province in which the two holy cities of Islam are located.

Freedom to follow on Moslem ground one's own habits and customs, and perform the rites and fulfil the duties of one's own religion.

Right of foreigners to be judged by the ambassadors and consuls of their respective governments in suits both civil and criminal, between one another, and the obligation of the local authorities to render aid to the consul in enforcing his decision and judgment concerning the same.

Inviolability of foreigners' domiciles and, in event of

urgent necessity for arresting a delinquent, obligation of government officials not to enter the dwelling-place of a foreigner without having previously notified the ambassador or consul, and unless accompanied by him or his deputy.

These statements are sufficient to show that merchant, traveler, and missionary in Turkey are there as foreigners, and as such they and their domiciles are under foreign protection. They have the privilege of holding property and of buying and selling the same. Mission Boards and foreign companies, being foreign corporations, cannot hold property in the empire. All property real and personal is held in the name of an individual. Exception is made in the case of the schools which have a firman (imperial irade) or which have obtained formal recognition from the sultan, in which case the institution itself holds the property in its own name, being a recognized chartered institution.

It is well that the missionary and merchant have been and still are independent of the Turkish officials, for, with the ignorance of those in the interior and their readiness to play into the hands of every rival or persecuting agency, there would be constant liability to arrest, imprisonment, and even deportation. In spite of the extra-territorial laws, missionaries and merchants repeatedly have been put under arrest for imaginary charges, and otherwise officially annoyed. These difficulties have been met in quietness and overcome without loss of position or prestige. In no instance has a missionary been arrested for an actual crime or misdemeanor. The usual charge against them is that they are plotting against the government, and the officers make attempts to search their houses for documentary evidence and for arms. These various evidences of hostility have not seemed to strain the generally friendly relations existing between the missionaries and the local governments.

Perhaps it should be stated here that all foreign capital invested in the country is held in the same way and has the same foreign protection. This is true of all Catholic institutions, Russian churches, monasteries, and schools, German orphanages, and mercantile warehouses, English residences, and stores, — everything that belongs to foreigners representing foreign capital is under foreign protection.

At the same time it is recognized that the school, hospital, or church which occupies one of these foreign buildings is a foreign institution and as such has, according to the Turkish capitulations, special immunities and privileges. All dealings with the Turkish government, even to the present time, are based upon this supposition. This does not seem strange or unnatural to the Turkish government, which permits the English, German, French, Austrian, and other governments to have their own post-offices at Constantinople, Smyrna, and other ports, in which they sell only their own postage-stamps and conduct all the postal business they can procure.

Under treaty rights above quoted, every concession or privilege granted by the sultan to the schools, churches, hospitals, or institutions belonging to England, France, Russia, or any other country, belongs by right to American institutions. The fact that America was discriminated against in this respect for many years, and that American institutions were thus deprived of privileges and concessions which had been conceded to similar institutions of several European powers, is well known, both at Constantinople, and in the United States. Happily these matters have now been adjusted.

After seven years of negotiations, in 1907 the sultan finally conceded in a formal manner the same rights and privileges to American institutions in his dominion which had already been granted to similar institutions of France, Russia, Germany and other countries; but as yet in most cases this concession exists largely in form, while the actual enjoyment of the privileges is withheld. At the same time insuperable obstacles are thrown in the way of the purchase of real estate by Americans and they are even forbidden to improve property which they have already acquired. It is only by eternal vigilance that American interests in Turkey can be safeguarded.

RELIGIOUS TOLERATION

ONE distinctive feature of Islam in Turkey — and this applies to nearly all Moslem races in the Ottoman empire except the Arabs — is that the Turk does not know the language of his sacred book. The Koran is as much a sealed book to the Turk as the Bible is to the peasant Roman Catholic of Central Europe. He knows, even if he is a peasant, many Arabic words and phrases, but although he may read the Koran, he cannot understand it; and it is, to the Mohammedan, a greater impiety to attempt to translate the Koran from the Arabic, than it was, till recent years, in the eyes of the faithful but ignorant Romanist to translate the Latin Bible into French or German. This ignorance of Arabic is a fact even among the more or less educated Turks of the capital and coast cities. It is very rare to find one who can read Arabic intelligently, and who speaks it correctly. Some years ago, when K—— Effendi, a learned Arab Koord, who had embraced Christianity, was called before the highest Mohammedan court, his perfect knowledge of the Arabic, of the Koran and of Mohammedan law and traditions completely confounded and silenced those who would have been his judges. — From "The Mohammedan World of To-day."

XXIV. RELIGIOUS TOLERATION

AT the beginning of mission work in Turkey the government and high officials seemed indifferent. They looked upon missionaries as only another sect of Christians. It apparently did not occur to them that Christians would attempt to present the claims of their religion to Moslems, or that there was the least probability that any Mohammedan would listen to a Christian upon the subject of religion. For centuries no Christian in Turkey had made any such attempt. Indeed, the lives of the Christians there exhibited little that was attractive in the religion of Jesus Christ.

The Turks, therefore, appeared to assume that the missionary movement was an effort to reform the Christians or to divide and weaken them. To either of these purposes or results the sultan and his officers saw no objections. To the Turks all who are not Moslems are infidels, and it mattered little to them what these believed since they denied faith in Mohammed.

Contrary to expectations, observing Moslems were attracted by the fact that the Protestants made use of neither pictures nor images in their worship, and demanded purity of life, honesty, temperance, and truthfulness in their adherents. This was to them a new phase of Christianity, one that accorded more with the Mohammedan ideas than the practises of the Catholic and Oriental Churches with which they were familiar. Among the early inquirers there were many Mohammedans. In 1835 Dr. Goodell of Constantinople wrote, " Almost every day I am visited by Mohammedans. I could very profitably devote my whole time to them." In cases not a few, in the early days, the Turkish officials were not slow to shield the evangelical Christians from the persecutions of the officials of the old Churches. As it did not occur to the sultan that there was any danger that Moslems could look with favor upon Christianity, he was the more free to grant full religious liberty under the importunity of Lord Stratford de Redcliffe, the British ambassador.

It was not, therefore, a difficult matter for Sultan Abdul Medjid to issue, November 3, 1839, an imperial rescript named the *Hatti Sherif of Gul Hane,* promising to protect the life, honor, and property of all his subjects irrespective of race or religion. At that time the sultan was eager to enlist and hold the sympathy of European rulers, and believed that such a concession would materially help toward it. This directly pledged the protection of the imperial government to every subject of the empire in the exercise of his rights as a citizen, without regard to religion or sect. It was the first declaration of the Turkish government putting Christians upon a parity with Mohammedans before the law. It was a long forward step in the way of administrative reform.

In August, 1843, an Armenian youth, some twenty years of age, was beheaded in the streets of Constantinople and his body exposed for three days, because he had once declared himself a Moslem and then later recanted. It seems that through fear of punishment this young man had accepted Islam and left the country. Later he returned and resumed the practises of his former religion. In spite of threats and promises, he adhered to his ancestral faith with the above results. Sir Stratford de Redcliffe did all in his power to save his life, but without success.

This execution aroused the ambassadors of England,

RELIGIOUS TOLERATION

France, Russia, and Prussia, who united in a formal demand upon the sultan to abolish the death penalty for a change of religion. Hitherto, there had been full liberty to change any and all non-Moslem religions, and for any one to abandon the faith of his fathers and to embrace Islam, but the right had been denied to a Mohammedan to depart from that faith.

Under pressure brought to bear by the four named ambassadors, led by the British, the sultan on the twenty-first of March, 1844, gave a written pledge as follows: " The Sublime Porte engages to take effectual measures to prevent, henceforward, the persecution and putting to death of the Christian who is an apostate." Two days later Abdul Medjid, in a conference with Sir Stratford, gave assurance " that henceforward neither shall Christianity be insulted in my dominions, nor shall Christians be in any way persecuted for their religion." The giver of these pledges was not only the sultan of Turkey, but he was also the caliph of the Mohammedan world. The year 1844 is memorable in Turkey and among the Mohammedans for this record of concessions in the interests of religious liberty in Turkey, and for all races, including Moslems.

In 1847 the Protestants had no standing in the Turkish empire. Nominally they were under the protection of the patriarch at Constantinople, but in fact they were without protection since their formal excommunication from the Old Church in the previous year. When their separation had been made complete, it was necessary that some recognition be secured for them from the sultan himself in order that they might continue to live in the empire. Through the British ambassador negotiations were carried on which resulted in the issuance of a firman by the grand vizier declaring that " Christian subjects of the Ottoman government professing Protestantism shall constitute a separate community with all the rights and privileges belonging to others," and that " no interference whatever be permitted in their temporal or spiritual concerns on the part of the patriarch, monks, or priests of other sects." This Protestant charter of 1847, as it was called, covered all Protestants who should change from the ancient Churches, but seemed studiously to avoid giving recognition to the possibility of Moslems accepting Protestantism. This charter was not issued with the imperial authority of the sultan, but only under the ministerial authority of the Porte. It was, therefore, liable to appeal at any time by either the sovereign or any succeeding ministry. In November, 1850, the reigning sultan, Abdul Medjid, granted an imperial charter to the Protestants confirming their distinct organization as a civil community and guaranteeing them religious rights and privileges equal to those granted all other religious organizations.

This secured *in perpetuum* to the Protestants the right to choose their own political chief, to transact business, to worship, to marry, to bury, and to perform all the functions of a religious organization under imperial protection. This was the Magna Charta of Protestantism in Turkey, and is called " The Imperial Protestant Charter of 1850." This was supplemented in 1853 by an imperial firman which was sent to all governors in the provinces, as well as to the head men of the Protestant communities, requiring that the charter of 1850 be strictly enforced. The above were issued in the interests of the Protestants alone.

Besides the written pledge of the sultan given to the ambassadors in 1844, there was no charter in Turkey insuring religious liberty to Mohammedans, except as the above mentioned Protestant charters admitted of such an interpretation. That was indefinite and, it was feared, did not guarantee safety to a Mohammedan who should change his faith. The European nations had demanded that the death penalty for Moslems upon changing their religion should be abolished.

In February, 1856, Sultan Medjid issued what is called the Magna Charta of religious liberty in Turkey. It is entitled the Hatti Sherif (Sacred Edict) or Hatti Humayoun (Imperial Edict). It was regarded at that time as guaranteeing full religious liberty to all Turkish subjects of every creed and faith. One sentence reads, "No subject of my empire shall be hindered in the exercise of the religion that he professes, nor shall he be in any way annoyed on this account. No one shall be compelled to change his religion." Lord Stratford assumed in his correspondence with his government that hereafter no one was to be molested on account of his religion or punished "whatever form of faith he denies."

This imperial charter was recognized by Great Britain, France, Austria, Russia, Sardinia, and Turkey, through their representatives who met in Paris in the same year to form the Treaty of Paris, to which body it was communicated by "His Imperial Majesty, the Sultan" and as "emanating spontaneously from his own will." However, it was clearly understood that no right was conceded to the above named Powers "to interfere either collectively or separately in the relations of His Majesty, the Sultan, with his subjects nor in the internal administration of his empire." This left Turkey the only interpreter of the document, and as sovereign in the administration of her own internal affairs, including the actual granting of religious liberty.

The acts of government and the behavior of Turkish officials at that period gave the impression that the Porte meant to recognize and enforce the principles of religious liberty. Many Mohammedans began openly to purchase copies of the Turkish Bible and to examine the claims of Christianity. In September, 1857, officials of the government in Constantinople carefully examined a Turkish gentleman, Selim Effendi, and his wife, and gave a certificate that they had become Christians without compulsion, and that " it was the will of His Majesty, the Sultan, that every Ottoman subject, without exception, should enjoy entire religious freedom." The spirit of inquiry spread and a converted Turk was employed as an evangelist in Constantinople and was unhindered in his labors among his countrymen.

In 1858 religious meetings were held with Turks and Koords in Eastern Turkey. In 1859 it was reported that the Turkish governors of Sivas, Diarbekr, and Cæsarea, after considering cases of the conversion of Moslems to Christianity, declared publicly that a Mohammedan who became a Christian would not be molested. In 1860 cases were reported from the Taurus Mountains of converted Moslems, and of others who were attendant upon Christian services. One of these was a member of the governor's council. In the vicinity of Aintab, at that time, some thirty Mohammedans were in attendance upon Christian services at one outstation. There were conversions of Turks reported at Diarbekr, Harpoot, and Cæsarea, followed by baptism, and without disturbance.

Up to 1860 fifteen Moslem converts had been baptized at Constantinople. One of these was a Turkish imam or preacher. In an examination before the Minister of War this imam declared that there were forty Turks in the city who believed as he did. This spirit of inquiry was widespread and continued until 1864. There was no doubt that Christian ideals were spreading rapidly among the Turks, and it is thought that the government formed the opinion that a considerable number of Mohammedans were desirous of reforming their own faith. Sultan Abdul Aziz became suspicious and fearful, and set spies to watch the missionaries. On a Sunday morning in Pera, Constantinople, Selim Effendi, a Turkish evangelist, and some twenty Turks were arrested as they emerged from their places of worship and were cast into prison. Without trial some of these men were sent into exile.

The official French paper, the *Journal de Constantinople*, in its issue of August 4, 1864, published a leader supposed to emanate from Ali Pasha, the grand vizier, in which the arrest of the Christian Turks was charged to the alleged fact that the zeal of the missionaries in making converts amounted to a "veritable war," and that in this work of proselyting seductive arts were employed. These charges were investigated by the Minister of the United States, and by the British ambassador, and not only were the missionaries exonerated from all blame, but Earl Russell, the Secretary of State for Foreign Affairs in Great Britain, strongly defended the missionaries and demanded of Turkey that she maintain in her dealings with her subjects the observance of the true principles of religious liberty. Upon the demand of the English government the exiled Turks were permitted to return.

It was at once understood by the Moslems that for them there was no liberty to change their faith. It is true that none were arrested upon the open charge of changing their religion, but every conceivable pretense was trumped up against them, to substantiate which any number of Mohammedan witnesses could be procured, and the Christian Mohammedan was sent into exile, languished in prison, or disappeared from view. Frequently missionaries attempted to follow up a case of manifest persecution, but they usually came upon a medical certificate that the man had died in prison from fever or some other natural cause, or lost all traces of the prisoner through frequent transfers to distant parts. Some men are known to have been shot by their guard in the transfer.

In the Treaty of Berlin, entered into in 1878 by England, Austria, Russia, France, Italy, and Turkey, Article 2 states that absolute religious liberty is to exist in all the various territories mentioned in the preceding article "including the whole Turkish empire." The sixty-second article begins, "The Sublime Porte, having expressed its willingness to maintain the principle of religious liberty and to give it the widest sphere, the contracting parties take cognizance of this spontaneous declaration." Then follow specifications of how the sultan is to carry out these principles.

In spite of these reiterated declarations, it is evident that the Turkish government does not and never did intend to acknowledge the right of a Moslem to become a Christian. A high official once told the writer that Turkey gives to all her subjects the widest religious liberty. He said, "There is the fullest liberty for the Armenian to become a Catholic, for the Greek to become an Armenian, for the Catholic and Armenian to become Greeks, for any one of them to become Protestant, or for all to become Mohammedans. There is the fullest and completest religious liberty for all the subjects of this empire."

In response to the question, "How about liberty for the Mohammedan to become a Christian?" he replied,

RELIGIOUS TOLERATION

"That is an impossibility in the nature of the case. When one has once accepted Islam and become a follower of the Prophet he cannot change. There is no power on earth that can change him. Whatever he may say or claim cannot alter the fact that he is a Moslem still and must always be such. It is, therefore, an absurdity to say that a Moslem has the privilege of changing his religion, for to do so is beyond his power." For the last forty years the actions of the official and influential Turks have borne out this theory of religious liberty in the Ottoman empire. Every Moslem showing interest in Christian things takes his life in his hands. No protection can be afforded him against the false charges that begin at once to multiply. His only safety lies in flight.

THE MACEDONIAN QUESTION

Mr. G. B. Ravndal, until recently United States consul at Beirut, Syria, is an intelligent and sympathetic witness of the progress of events in that part of the Turkish empire. He writes, with special reference to the commercial aspects of missionary advance, that "the Syria of to-day cannot be compared with the Syria of twenty-five years ago. Education is working wonders, raising the standard of living, multiplying and diversifying the requirements of the people, developing the natural resources of the country, and increasing the purchasing capacity of the individual. Illiteracy is on the wane, independent thought is in the ascendant. We have printing-presses, railroads, carriage-roads, bridges, postal and telegraph routes. Trade is increasing in volume and variety, and the United States is getting a larger and larger share of it. Our country, owing primarily to the efforts of our missionaries, is near and dear to a large portion of the population, not only of this country, but of the entire Levant — nay, even of Persia and the Sudan. Through our college (at Beirut), with its School of Commerce and museums, through the mission press, the industrial academy, and the experimental farm, missionaries have become ambassadors of American trade, and as the foreign commerce of the Levant swells into larger proportions — it is yet in its infancy — the United States is getting a surer foothold in the near East." He also speaks of his gratification in witnessing the increasing introduction of American machinery into Syria, such as reaping, threshing, and milling machines, and expresses his confidence that "Western Asia will before long become a market for our agricultural, irrigation, and other machinery, which no manufacturer at home will despise or ignore." He refers to the School of Commerce recently established in connection with the American College at Beirut, with its students drawn from a widely extended region, reaching from Trebizond on the north to Khartum on the south, and from Albania in the west to Teheran in the east, as an enterprise which is destined to "play a leading part in the economics of the Levant." There is a business ring to testimonies like these just quoted from men of official position in the East, which surely cannot be credited to missionary partiality or misjudgment, and as such we are glad to have the privilege of presenting them. — James S. Dennis, in "Christian Missions and Social Progress."

XXV. THE MACEDONIAN QUESTION

THE Albanians in Macedonia have been for more than a generation a source of terror and a tower of strength to the Turkish government. They number perhaps two million in the country and occupy a region remote from the capital, and difficult to control. They have never been fully loyal to the sultan or any other ruler, and, occupying as they do the fastnesses of the mountains along the western borders of Macedonia, they have enjoyed unusual liberty. They have been referred to as the least civilized of the European races. They are warlike by inheritance and profession, and cling with an intense devotion to their Albanian tongue.

They claim that they are direct descendants from the ancient Pelasgi and are proud of their lineage. An Albanian prince told the writer not long since that he was of the same race that gave Alexander the Great to the world. They call themselves *Skipeter* or "the Eagle People." The majority of the race have outwardly accepted Mohammedanism but in most cases this is largely in form only. As the Koran is permitted to circulate in Turkey only in the Arabic tongue, and as few Albanians are acquainted with that language, they have little knowledge of Islam, and perhaps less love for it. Many of them are nominal members of the Greek Church.

On the other hand, the Turkish government, through the love of the Albanians for war, has brought many of them into direct service to the state. Some of the best and bravest officers in the Turkish army are Albanians. Mohammed Ali Pasha, who reformed Egypt and founded the present khedival house, was an Albanian. They have risen to the highest positions of influence and power in the empire, not a few of them serving in the sultan's cabinet. This reveals the native strength of this people, and the reason why the sultan jealously guards the race in his attempt to hold them true to Mohammedanism and loyal to himself. Their very strength of character makes them bold and fearless in the fastnesses of their remote mountain home, and hard to subdue; but when they declare allegiance to a cause or a person they cannot be diverted by fear or favor.

This sturdy people with high codes of honor in their dealings with each other and with strangers number about one-tenth of the Mohammedan population of the Turkish empire. Until within a few years they have been regarded as inaccessible to the missionary and to the Christian worker. Recently mission work in Macedonia has come into contact with them and a few have embraced Christianity. Nearly twenty years ago a school for girls was started in Kortcha, one of their chief cities, conducted by Albanian Christians, and in the Albanian language. Some of the chief men gladly put their daughters in the school, but were later compelled by the sultan to withdraw them.

The Albanians constitute one of the vital race problems of Macedonia. They are eager for modern education and are restless under the restrictive and oppressive rule of the Porte. If they become, as a race, members of the Greek Church, as many have already become, their influence will be cast against the rule of the sultan and in favor of outside protection. If the Turks can hold them to a servile Mohammedanism, they will greatly strengthen the power of the throne at Constantinople. Upon the other

THE MACEDONIAN QUESTION

hand, if they insist upon a modern education for their children, and enter upon an impartial investigation of the merits of Protestant Christianity, there is no standard for measuring their influences on the other races of Macedonia. Albanians in large numbers are coming to the United States, and here they seek education for themselves and plead eagerly for assistance that they may be able to give greater educational and religious privileges to their children at home.

This race is but a part of the Macedonian question which has been agitating Turkey and Europe for the past few years. If the demands of the European Powers are acceded to, the hold of the sultan upon Macedonia will be weakened, although not broken. It has been well known for the last twenty years that, with every weakening of the sultan's power, strength has never returned to it. Should there be a withdrawal of Turkish rule from Macedonia, including Albania, it would remove all restraint from the Albanians and give them full freedom to educate their children and to worship God according to the dictates of their consciences. Under these circumstances few would probably remain Mohammedans for any length of time. To Turkey these conditions contain mighty possibilities, nor are they without deep significance to the entire Moslem world. It may be that we are to-day witnessing a break in the Moslem ranks that have hitherto presented a solid wall of opposition to every Christian approach. There is no phase of the present Turkish question which is more important or significant.

Besides the Albanians, Macedonia has three most discordant national elements consisting of Turks, Bulgarians, and Greeks. The Bulgarians are eager for the extension of the Bulgarian principality south to the sea, while the

Greeks desire the extension of the kingdom of Greece eastward to include that part of Macedonia in which a large number of Greeks dwell. The Turks represent the government and are strenuously opposed to both these tendencies, and they express their opposition in every kind of repressive measure known to the Porte. To this is added the rivalry and hostile jealousies existing between the Greek and Bulgarian churches in the country, and the resultant condition of affairs is about as bad as well can be.

Marauding parties, formed and armed in many instances upon the Bulgarian side of the border, have penetrated into Macedonia, terrorizing all classes and clashing with the Turkish troops. These have operated for several years. The object of these expeditions apparently was to arouse the attention of the world to the misgovernment of the country and so secure outside intervention, and consequent reform. Their purpose has been offset by the lawlessness of the Turkish soldiers, and between the two the innocent citizen and peasant are ground almost to powder. There are also Greek bands of marauders who strike terror to the regions in which they operate.

It is to restore some degree of order and to prevent the country from running into absolute lawlessness, that the European Powers have endeavored to unite and secure for Macedonia a systematic and safe administration. If the Powers succeed in this effort, we may reasonably hope that the hold of Turkey upon Macedonia will soon begin to break and that ultimately all that section of Europe will be free of Turkish rule. The sultan will not yield those rich and fertile provinces of his empire willingly, but he is powerless to resist the demands of the combined Powers of Europe.

GENERAL POLITICAL SITUATION

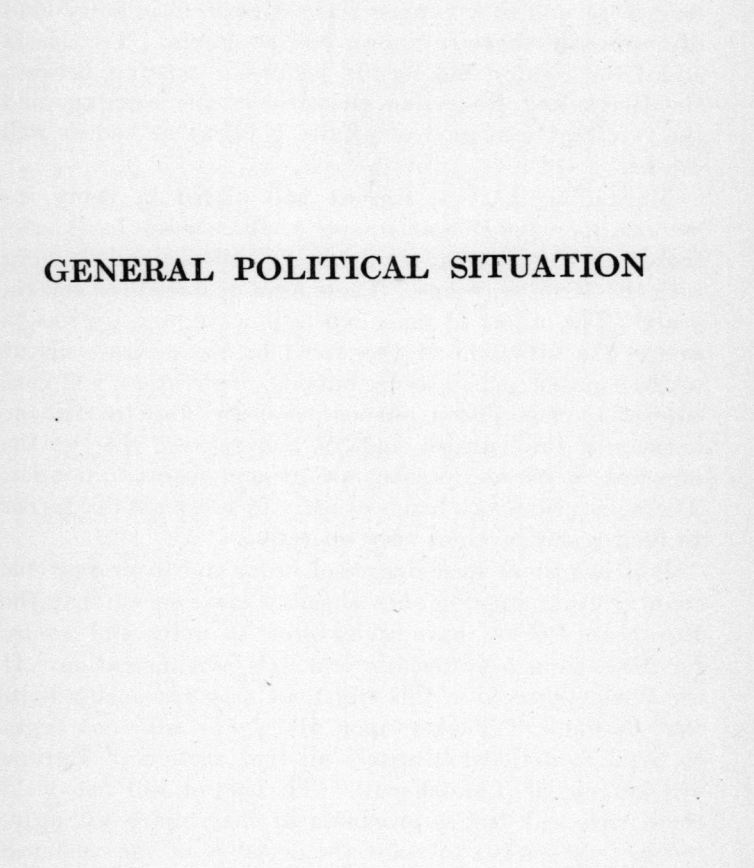

THERE are no indications of the presence of the "Young Turk" secret organization, but there is a growing discontent with the present régime. This is caused (1) by individual dissatisfaction with injustice, increased taxation and harsh military service; (2) by the racial ambition of Arabic-speaking Moslems who regard the Turk as a barbarian and of doubtful orthodoxy, and are restive under Turkish rule which allots them few positions, civil or military. Many Arabs wish the caliphate assumed by one of their race and would bring the capital of Islam near if not into Arabia, its cradle. This politico-religious aspiration is ascribed to Midhat Pasha and has been fostered, since his day, by pamphlets widely scattered and by secret societies. (3) Discontent also results from impotent rage at the waning political power of Islam under Turkish leadership. Moslem supremacy has been lost in Mount Lebanon, in most European provinces, in part of Asia Minor, in Cyprus, Crete, Egypt, and is now imperilled in North Africa. (4) Another cause of discontent is realization of the fact that universal corruption is sapping the vitality of the empire and dissipating its resources. (5) To these causes is added knowledge that other lands have secured improved material conditions and equable justice without interference with religious observances. This embitters by contrast their present situation. Emigration, which has taken tens of thousands of Christians from Syria, has lately begun to draw from the Moslems. The letters of the absent and the influence of those who have returned are factors of unrest. That any or all of these elements of political ferment will produce any revolt is improbable. No leader could expect success with an unarmed and poor set of followers nor could he unify and harmonize hostile sects. — From "The Mohammedan World of To-day."

XXVI. GENERAL POLITICAL SITUATION

THE political situation in Turkey can well be summed up as " A fifteenth century Oriental government in conflict with modern civilization." This condition is aggravated by the existence of European rivalries and jealousies and Mohammedan fanaticism. The combination of these forces is hard to analyze and its results even more difficult to forecast.

The first, and in some respects the most evident, difficulty especially manifest to those who reside in the empire, is the intellectual, social, and moral upheaval caused by the influence of Christian civilization upon the people as a whole. New and, to that country, startling ideas of religious freedom, human rights, and the true functions of a government, have taken hold upon large numbers out of every nationality and religion. So long as the government of Turkey is conducted according to Oriental fifteenth century ideals, it is inevitable that there must be a conflict, trying both to the government and to the governed. So long as the people were densely ignorant, knowing little of the world outside and far less of the principle that governs civilized people, they made little complaint. As enlightenment came to them from various sources, it was inevitable that unrest should also come. Had Turkey been able to adjust herself to the new situation and move forward in her administrative methods, keeping pace with the growing intelligence of her subjects, she might have become one of the strong, compact, and thrifty nations of the East.

She chose otherwise and began early to devise and put into execution plans for the suppression of general education. At the same time, the press was throttled by a severe censorship and all who were suspected of thinking for themselves came under a ban. Turkey, in her feeble way, attempted to follow the lead of Russia in this respect, and did so undoubtedly under Russian advice. The failure to protect property has discouraged the investment of capital. Industries languished and have almost died out. Inevitably enterprising men would seek to emigrate. When once outside the country few incline to return so long as present conditions continue. In fact, the government discourages the return of any who have been abroad, fearing the new ideas they acquired in Europe and the United States. At the present time the government practically forbids the return to Turkey of all who have been in civilized countries, endeavoring to maintain a wall of seclusion against all ideas of modern civilization. Turkey calls such people dangerous characters and throws them into prison as revolutionists.

This dangerous class includes Albanians, Turks, Greeks, Syrians, and Armenians. In most respects among these are found the most enlightened people of the country. Some of the educated Turks have obtained their new ideas from sources within the country, while others have studied in Europe. Many of them have come into more modern ideas of a government and its functions, and would gladly see changes made which would bring Turkey into harmony with Europe. These are called the new Turks, and are classified roughly together as the " New Turk party." They are not revolutionists in the ordinary sense of that word. They find no favor with the reigning sultan, and are exiled and even executed without trial. The party, al-

GENERAL POLITICAL SITUATION

though apparently not organized, is a fact, and the spirit of reform is spreading among the Turks. Measures to suppress this movement are generally secret and are seldom reported abroad. A Turk once told the writer that "when outrages are perpetrated against the Christians, the whole world lifts up its hands in horror and the sultan is ordered to cease; but when the poor Turks are the victims, where is there a voice raised in their defense?"

Naturally the Turkish government fears the Armenians since they have made such rapid progress in education during the last eighty years. Since Bulgaria became practically an independent state, Turkey has tightened its hold upon Armenia. At the same time, the Armenians, seeing the great freedom and prosperity enjoyed by the Bulgarians, have cherished dreams of the time when they too might be free. While all Armenians have at times indulged in such visions, but few have ever seriously considered the proposition a practicable one. Only the most rattle-headed of them declare such a plan possible and only such are advocating revolutionary measures to that end. Armenia (a name not permitted in Turkey) can hardly be erected into an independent nation, although it would be impossible to convince Sultan Hamid II of that fact. He governs as if he expected hourly that Armenia may rise and demand its freedom, although the Mohammedans are everywhere greatly in the majority.

There are, however, a considerable number of Armenians who have been driven to desperation by the injustice and cruelty of the government. Aware that they are powerless to reform Turkey, they declare their inability longer to endure. These resort to acts of desperation with the hope that Europe will become aroused, as it did in the case of Bulgaria, and interfere in the interests of the oppressed.

Small revolutionary parties called by various names have been organized in Macedonia, in Armenia, and especially in border countries like Bulgaria, Russia, and Persia, for the secretly avowed purpose of compelling the attention and interference of Europe. They have stirred the Turks to acts of extreme cruelty, but have egregiously failed to accomplish their purpose.

These internal affairs which disturb and vex the people almost beyond endurance are allowed to continue, unchecked by European interference, because the nations of Europe cannot agree to act together, nor can they trust any one to act for the rest. England's influence, which was supreme when the Treaty of Berlin was signed, has been superseded by Russia, and she in turn has taken, more recently, second place to Germany. The sultan, most astute of all, is able to set rivalry, jealousy, and suspicion against suspicion, jealousy and rivalry, and while they quarrel over methods and precedents, he works his will. No diplomat is able to cope with the sultan of Turkey, because his statements cannot be relied upon, while his promises are meaningless. Every ambassador and minister learns this to his sorrow, but is powerless to meet the conditions created by it. To call the sovereign of a state to which he is accredited " a falsifier " would not be diplomatic, and might strain existing relations, and to meet falsehood with falsehood is against the principles of representatives of the Christian nations. While the foreign legations are considering these problems the sultan continues his own way.

The present unsettled condition in Russia and the defeat of that country by the Japanese will undoubtedly weaken her influence over the sultan. The emperor of Germany, while maintaining friendly relations with Hamid II,

GENERAL POLITICAL SITUATION

does not seem to attempt to restrain him in his acts of violence against his own subjects. If he would, it is believed by many that Emperor William might accomplish much in bringing about reform measures in Turkey, if the other Powers of Europe would permit him to do so.

Financially Turkey seems to be upon the verge of bankruptcy. Her system of assessing taxes, paralyzing industry, and her method of often collecting from the poor taxpayer many times the amount due, have impoverished the country. The occasional general massacres in different sections have been terribly destructive to national wealth, striking directly at its sources. The strained political situation is due in no small measure to the economic conditions of that country, accompanied by the unjust administration of the government. If Turkey could afford her subjects of all classes a safe and just government, it might soon be one of the most prosperous and thrifty countries in Asia, comparing favorably with the governments of Europe.

What the future will bring forth for Turkey no one can predict. Some twelve years ago the writer asked an old and experienced diplomat at Constantinople what was to be the outcome of the then threatening conditions in the country. His reply was, "I have studied Turkey from within and without for thirty years, and have carefully weighed the diverse forces that are operating in the empire. I have come to one clear and final conclusion which I am certain will stand the test of time, and that is that I do not know anything about what the future will produce here."

One thing is sure, the methods of government which were successful there six centuries ago cannot be continued indefinitely. Modern thought and ideas will not submit in patience and quietness forever to the oppressive measures of the middle ages. Dawn is breaking and it is useless for the night to rail at its coming. Intelligent belief will win in the end, and justice and righteousness must triumph. This may cost the shedding of blood, but indications do not point that way. A mighty revolution is already in progress which will accomplish its purpose, in time, by the simple laws of God wrought out by the lives and acts of intelligent and righteous men. The forces of reform are in operation, not only in institutions, but in the hearts and in the longings, and in the purposes, of men of all classes and races. It propagates itself as it moves from coast to coast, and from plain to mountain fastness, gaining in force and depth and breadth with every decade. Present conditions cannot indefinitely continue. Times may be worse before they are better, but even greater changes are inevitable and at no remotely distant day. God is in his heavens and he is guiding the affairs of the Turkish empire.

CONSTITUTIONAL GOVERNMENT

IN the Mohammedan dominions of Turkey missionary institutions have graduated men who have in many instances occupied government positions on account of their superior capabilities, in spite of the fact that Christian officials are greatly handicapped by Moslem prejudices. In the case of the Bulgarian graduates of Robert College, it was said in 1902, by a missionary of the American Board then residing at Sofia, that "since the beginning of the national administration of Bulgaria, in 1878, there has been no government ministry without one at least, and often two or three, Robert College members. The present Secretary of the Cabinet, whose ability has preserved his position for him during ten years, and under eight successive ministries, is one of these men." The judge of the supreme court, besides the mayor of Sofia, and many others in diplomatic, judicial, or clerical posts, are all Robert College men. The Syrian Protestant College at Beirut has graduated men who, as government appointees, occupy positions of responsibility, and exert no little influence in the administration of political and judicial affairs in Syria, especially in the Mount Lebanon government. Its medical graduates, moreover, are to be found in the military and civil service in almost all sections of Asiatic Turkey, and notably under the Egyptian administration. — JAMES S. DENNIS in "Christian Missions and Social Progress."

MANY causes have combined, many factors are present, many influences have turned the hearts of men through that empire [Turkey]; but if we ask ourselves what the governing and final factor is which has brought about the first of the world's bloodless revolutions, which has seen a people divided and dissevered by creed, by race, by language, by every conceivable difference which can separate the sons and daughters of men, suddenly act together — we do ill if we forget that for eighty years the American missionaries have been laying the foundations and preaching the doctrine which makes free government possible. — TALCOTT WILLIAMS, LL.D., editor Philadelphia Press, in an address at Brooklyn, N. Y., Oct. 15, 1908.

XXVII. CONSTITUTIONAL GOVERNMENT

LATE in 1902 a plan for administrative reform in the Adrianople, Salonica, and Monastir Provinces of European Turkey was published. These included Macedonia where disorders and atrocities had become chronic. Under this measure the valis or governors were given new powers and an inspector general was appointed reporting directly to the grand vizier. The Powers compelled the addition of a financial commission representing them, which should examine the budget of the three vilayets and recommend improvements. With the aid of three Ottoman inspectors, the commission was to supervise the provincial finances and in other ways bring relief to the untoward conditions of the inhabitants. The gendarmerie was put under a foreign officer with an Italian general in command, and much improved in efficiency.

A three per cent increase in the customs duties provided funds for securing other reforms. These, however, it must be said, existed largely upon paper. While the Powers ostensibly had some responsibility and authority in the administration of affairs in Macedonia, the sultan was able in ways so well known to himself to thwart their exercise of it while the discordant elements in Albania and Macedonia made conditions for all classes more intolerable than ever.

Again, early in 1908, the Powers gave hesitating attention to this plague-spot of Europe as one united cry of distress arose from all tongues, the Turkish, Greek, Bulgarian, and Albanian alike. It is impossible to say which race was the greatest sufferer or which the freest from oppression. Practically the entire country was in a state of anarchy and there was none to deliver. On March 13, 1908, the Porte reluctantly consented to the British proposal that the mandates of foreign officials in Macedonia be renewed for a period of seven years. A budget was adopted for the support of the army, the civil list, and the railway, which threatened a deficit of nearly $4,000,000. With all these arrangements no party to the transaction was satisfied, except those European Powers that hoped, in the end, to make political capital out of Macedonia's affliction. These entered reluctantly into agreement as did also the sultan, who saw his personal power in the three provinces gradually wane; but his former experiences made him quick to read the signs of the times.

In the meantime the army in those provinces had been reenforced. Monastir, upon the border of Albania and connected by rail with Salonica, was made an important military post. The people themselves had no faith that these measures would assure them of safety of life and property, while the representatives of the Porte were anxious to demonstrate that the scheme of the Powers was not calculated to restore and maintain order. Matters went on from intolerable to worse until plunder, robbery, brigandage and murder became daily occurrences in practically all parts of the country. These were the conditions that prevailed in Macedonia the latter part of July, 1908.

What were some of the general conditions in Turkey which led directly to the uprising in Macedonia soon after the 20th of July, 1908, resulting in the revival of the constitution for all Turkey which had remained inactive since 1877? Sultan Hamid II has been an absolute ruler. His pride has centered in his complete personal mastery over every department of government and all officials, both civil and military. As he advanced in years, he became increasingly suspicious of every one holding office or occupying a position of influence. He seemed so morbidly afraid of a popular uprising that any mention of an Armenian revolution or reference to a constitutional government or suggestion of a Young or New Turkey party, threw him into a state of nervous panic. In order to protect his own person, to guard his administration from corruption by men who thought in terms of modern government, and to suppress any and all movements toward reform, he gradually built up about him a cumbersome, cruel and expensive system of espionage. Every official from the grand vizier at the Porte to the postmaster in a remote inland village was watched and reported upon. One official was directed to make secret reports upon a colleague and all men of wealth and consequent influence, and especially all who had received a degree of modern education were always under sleepless surveillance from the watch-dogs of the palace.

No one knows how many of these men were engaged in the secret service, but there were undoubtedly many thousands. Some drew salaries of large proportion while others were paid according to the service rendered. These spies well knew that they too were under observation by others who had been commissioned to see that they were loyal to their chief. The gates of the foreign embassies were guarded, and the names of all Ottoman subjects who entered them were reported to the police. Everywhere these sleuth-hounds of Yildez were doing their best to justify their appointment, and, if possible, to secure a rise in salary or a handsome bonus. It is reported that this large corps of secret service men were the only officials who received liberal pay and who got it regularly and in cash.

DAYBREAK IN TURKEY

Through information thus obtained, strange things took place. Of course there were never any hearings or trials. None were necessary when trusted spies had reported adversely. Groups of students in the government schools disappeared and the parents even did not dare ask a question. Men of wealth found themselves bundled off to Arabia in poverty, and officials in honor on one day were in exile, if not in their graves, on the next. The only thing certain about the life of an influential and intelligent Ottoman subject was his being under strict surveillance by those who were mainly concerned to satisfy their chief of their own efficiency.

During recent years the one horror of the sultan has been the "Young Turks," which meant Turkish subjects who know about good government and are eager to see it tried in Turkey. All who were suspected of harboring such ideas were summarily treated. Many such have been banished into interior provinces such as Macedonia, Asia Minor, Armenia and Syria. Some were given minor offices in their place of banishment, but all have been diligent in promoting their ideas. There is hardly a town of importance in Turkey to which one or more of these intelligent, thinking Ottoman subjects has not been exiled and where they have not propagated their principles of reform as opportunity offered. This seed-sowing of modern ideas has been broadcast, and the seed has fallen into rich soil. During these years, secretly and in the dark, multitudes of Ottoman subjects have been studying the science of government with the best educated in the empire as instructors. The lesson has not been the less impressive because secret and the teacher none the less in earnest because his profession was perilous. Wherever these exiles went they found the people writhing under injustice. Excessive

CONSTITUTIONAL GOVERNMENT

taxes were assessed and then collected by extortionate officials who, in the name of the sultan, carried on a system of public robbery. Taxes paid in the spring were again demanded in the autumn, the peasant having no defense in the absence of tax receipts. These teachers of a possible new order of things did not need to take time to persuade their hearers that a change was desirable. Restlessness, approaching a state of sheer desperation, everywhere prevailed. In the meantime, revolutionary committees or organizations among Armenians and perhaps other nationalities had identified themselves sympathetically, if not formally, with the New Turkey party.

Government by espionage and instruction of the masses by banished reformers have been going on in all parts of Turkey for many years, no one can say with certainty how many. It was inevitable that a crisis must come. The additional fact that all public officials, especially the army, were poorly paid on paper, if at all, brought things to a pass that seemed to be waiting only for a leader or an occasion to precipitate concerted action.

Such was the situation in Macedonia the latter part of July, 1908. The large army, half starved and underpaid, was sent into the country to put down lawlessness among a people made desperate by prolonged oppression. Previous experiences had satisfied the soldiers that in battling with the hardy mountaineers, many of whom were fighting for their homes, they had little chance of success. Why should they throw their lives away in a useless conflict with people of their own blood, and for a sovereign who appeared scarcely grateful. This was indeed an opportune hour to strike a blow for liberty. It is not yet known how completely the New Turks — called in Macedonia, the "Committee of Ottoman Union and Progress" — had organized, but subsequent events show an excellent degree of cooperation.

In Monastir the army took oath of allegiance to this committee; the troops in Salonica, Kortcha and other parts of the country followed in their lead. A few officers who hesitated were summarily shot. Proclamations in the name of the committee were posted in the leading cities asking all to join the society. At Kortcha in Albania, for instance, a time limit was set for joining the movement, after which all outside were to be regarded as traitors. In all Macedonia there seemed to be little hesitation. Other proclamations enjoining orderly conduct were posted, and within five days Macedonia was more quiet and life and property safer than for twenty years previously.

In the meantime, the leaders were in telegraphic communication with the sultan at Constantinople. What had taken place was reported to him, and he was asked to declare a constitutional government without delay. It was intimated that the army was ready to march on Constantinople if he refused. He hesitated for a while, but when he learned that the Albanians were in the forefront of the movement, and that he could not depend upon the troops, he yielded to a demand he could not resist. Ferid Pasha, his Albanian grand vizier, was summarily dismissed. Said Pasha was appointed to succeed him and Kiamil Pasha was placed upon the Council of Ministers; both men of liberal ideas who had been saved by Great Britain when there was a price upon their heads. Stormy debates followed in the palace at Constantinople as to what could be done to meet the demands of the formidable committee in Macedonia. Honeyed words and paper promotions had proved unavailing and repeated telegrams from the front spoke of

CONSTITUTIONAL GOVERNMENT

urgency. At last the sultan yielded and, on Friday, the 24th of July, issued an irade restoring the constitution of 1876 that had been suspended since 1877.

The constitution which is now revived was sanctioned by Sultan Hamid II soon after he came to the throne in 1876. At that time a European Commission met in Constantinople to suggest methods by which the sultan might set in order his European provinces. He desired to show Europe that he was able to work out reforms of his own. He therefore appointed a well-recognized reformer as grand vizier and proclaimed a constitution. This provided for a responsible ministry, a senate, a chamber of deputies, the right of public meeting, freedom of the press, the appointment of judges for life, compulsory intermediate education, religious liberty, and a long list of other rights and privileges belonging to an enlightened and free government. Within two months, Midhat Pasha, who drafted the constitution, was banished.

An election, however, was held and, in 1877, the Senate and the Chamber of Deputies met in a Parliament House that had been fitted up by the sultan in Constantinople. At that time in his speech from the throne, he repeated his promise for social reforms and a reorganization of the army and navy. The two houses were discussing this address when war broke out in Russia. Martial law was proclaimed in May, and in June parliament was adjourned. Once again that year it was assembled but the sultan was not pleased with the independence exhibited, so in February, 1878, it was dissolved or "suspended" as he preferred to call it. It never met again.

This is the constitution to which the thoroughly alarmed sultan turned as the demand came up from his trusted troops, beloved Albanians and faithful Moslems in Macedonia, for immediate and effectual reforms.

To this he solemnly swore fidelity in the most sacred way known to the Moslem, namely, upon the Koran. The Sheik-ul-Islam, the supreme high priest of the Mohammedan faith, exhibited to the people in Constantinople the book upon which this oath was taken, and made public declaration that it is the purpose of the sultan faithfully to carry out his pledge. He even went further than this and said that it is the spirit of Islam to give the fullest religious freedom to all subjects of the empire and to guarantee constitutional justice and liberty. All this committed the sultan to the constitution far more irrevocably than he was committed in 1876. It made also the Sheik-ul-Islam witness and sponsor to the people of the sultan's promise.

The announcement that a constitutional government was granted was wired to the impatient leaders in Macedonia and published in the papers in Constantinople. The result was unparalleled in the history of any country in any age. All Turkey gave way to a carnival of joy. An order was issued abolishing the secret service, and freedom of the press was guaranteed by the constitution. All political prisoners were released and those in exile were invited back to their homes. Incidentally the prison doors were thrown wide open and the criminal shared the common joy of all. The occupation of the censors of the press was gone and every paper in the empire spread the glad news that a new day had dawned. New papers started like mushrooms in a night. Representatives from the committee in Macedonia proceeded to Constantinople and apparently came to an understanding with the sultan as to the situation. He was plainly told, it is persistently rumored, that if he did not appoint as ministers men of their choosing, his only safety would lie in abdication. The old members of the cabinet, representing the régime of oppression, disappeared or were imprisoned, and the new men quietly stepped into their places. Isset Pasha, the much hated secretary of the sultan, in spite of efforts by the new party to retain him, succeeded in boarding a British vessel at Constantinople and escaping to England.

The people of Turkey, with centuries of repressive discipline in the political school of the empire, were supposed to have lost the faculty of spontaneous exultation or general demonstration of joy. But impelled by a sense of liberty never before experienced, the entire population broke into an outburst of appreciation for the new order of things such as Turkey had never before witnessed.

The people gathered by thousands and by tens of thousands in the public squares of their cities to listen to the proclamation of liberty and the firing of salutes in honor of the occasion. These crowds were composed of Christians and Moslems, who only a few days before had seemed to hate each other with deadliest hatred. Now they clapped their hands and joined their voices in shouting "Long live the Fatherland," "Long live the People," "Long live Liberty," "Long live the Constitution." Christian and Moslem leaders embraced and kissed one another in public while tears rolled down the cheeks of thousands as they took part in the festivities. Great assemblies were addressed by Mohammedan and Christian speakers, all of whom exhorted the people to unity and the maintenance of order, declaring that religious distinctions were now done away, as all pledged their allegiance to the new constitution and to the Ottoman empire. In an immense procession in Salonica a float was drawn upon which rode a girl dressed as the Goddess of Liberty. At Constantinople in one of the large Gregorian churches, the assembly was addressed by both Mohammedans and Christians and the Moslem band played the Armenian national air. For an Armenian to have sung this air one month before would have meant exile or death.

In one of the principal mosques of the capital a memorial service for the Armenians slain in the massacre of 1896 was held in which Moslems and Christians fraternally joined. This was followed by a similar mass meeting in an Armenian church in memory of the Mohammedans who had laid down their lives for the freedom of their country. All united in the declaration that the massacred Armenians and the Moslems dying in exile were brothers in their common sacrifice for the freedom of Turkey.

These scenes of spontaneous celebration enacted in the great centers of population indicated the universal readiness of the people for the proclamation and their unanimity in the reforms. It is indeed an uprising of the people for liberty and, by meeting their demands, the sultan, for the time, has made himself the most popular ruler sitting upon any throne. The carnival of joy gives hint of what their disappointment will be should there be any breach of good faith in securing to them all the privileges granted by the constitution. Not the least of their joy is in the marvel that this revolution has been brought about almost without the shedding of blood. A few in Macedonia who hesitated to join the new party were executed, but in Constantinople there was no loss of life in completing the transfer from the old to the new régime.

The masses of Turkey know little of the duties and responsibilities of a parliament. They are launching out upon an experiment, unknown and untried. It remains

CONSTITUTIONAL GOVERNMENT

to be seen how they will meet their own expectations in the measure of self-government which the constitution grants. There are many able, educated men among the Turks, Armenians, Greeks, Bulgarians, and Albanians. The question is: Will these, laying aside all national and religious jealousies, be able to work together in the creation of a new government, and all under the leadership of Sultan Hamid? It is also an open question whether the sultan himself, after a life of absolutism, can adapt himself to the new order and execute it in a way to insure a sympathetic following and substantial success.

There is danger that the people may be unreasonable in their demands and rebel against the collection of taxes adequate for the proper conduct of the government. Only a beginning has yet been made. Much remains to be done.

In all the history of Turkey a reform has never been inaugurated with the same solemnity and religious sanction that attended the recent declaration of constitutional government. The highest sanction of Islam has been accorded it, and, so far as we can see, the sultan could not materially alter his course without bringing himself personally in the eyes of the people into open conflict with his own religion and the faith of the great majority of his subjects. It is conceivable that, if he should find it impossible faithfully to carry out the provisions of the constitution, he will be asked to step aside and permit his constitutionally proclaimed successor to fulfil his oath of loyalty.

Under a constitutional government well established and righteously administered, there are boundless possibilities for the material, intellectual, political, and moral advance of the empire, so long regarded as decadent. This can be accomplished only by tireless labors and great sacrifices upon the part of those who bear the responsibility. But it can be done if all national and traditional differences are buried in the one patriotic purpose to restore the country to something of its former power and glory, and to weld the masses of its divergent population into a homogeneous nation.

It is to be sincerely hoped that the European Powers will not interfere with this endeavor upon the part of the people of Turkey to establish for themselves a safe and just government. They have the right to a free hand in working out the problem of government for themselves, so long as they do not plunge the country into anarchy.

There has never been a time when Western peoples have had a greater opportunity to aid materially in making stable the new order of things in the Ottoman empire. Under the Constitution, with compulsory education and a free press, Turkey will require aid from without in organizing and establishing schools all over the country, and in the preparation of a literature of the widest range. These needs are at once apparent. The colleges in the country should be immediately enlarged and strengthened that they may be able to meet the demands that will be made upon them. The entire country is in need of normal schools to train teachers for educational institutions of the preparatory grades. Turkey needs and deserves the sympathy and cooperation of other nations, not by way of interference, but by way of fraternal assistance and genuine help to the full realization of all the benefits of a representative and a constitutional government. The motto which seems to have been adopted by common consent is, "Liberty, Justice, Equality and Fraternity."

CONSTITUTIONAL GOVERNMENT

Every friend of constitutional government can sympathetically join with the people of Turkey in their honest endeavor to establish a new order for themselves upon these four corner-stones as their basis of union and mutual well-being.

THE CONSTITUTION VINDICATED

"WHAT does this revolution signify to us and to our work in Turkey? It does not promise everything which we might wish, but it does offer far more than we had any reason to expect from the Turks. So far as its aims are *political*, it seeks to save and strengthen the dominion of the Ottoman Turks. So far as it is *religious*, it seeks to uphold and extend the influence of *Islam* in the world by grafting into it social and political principles which are Christian in their origin and historical development. So far as we are concerned, it sets before us an open door with free speech, a free press, religious liberty, and the chance to exert all our influence to help the people of all races to fit themselves for freedom and constitutional government. It invites us to do with all our might what we have been trying to do for three-quarters of a century.

"It is our great opportunity. For the time at least all opposition to our work has ceased. It is well understood that we have no selfish ends in view and do not covet anything which belongs to Turkey — our colleges, our hospitals, our schools, our printing-press are all devoted to the elevation of the people in their material, intellectual, social, moral, and religious lives. If we have accomplished great things under the adverse conditions of the past, we have every reason to hope for greater things in the future." — Rev. GEORGE WASHBURN, D.D., LL.D., For forty years President of Robert College, Constantinople.

XXVIII. THE CONSTITUTION VINDICATED

AFTER the first flush of exultation had passed in the port cities of Turkey and the interior vilayets were assured that a new régime had been established throughout the country, preparations began to be made, under instructions from the capital, for the holding of a general election. The constitution called for a senate appointed by the sultan and a house of representatives elected by the people. Probably in no country did preparations for recording the wishes of the voters assume a more solemn and serious aspect than they did throughout Turkey. In many sections the ballot-box was shown almost the respect that is accorded the altar in some of the Oriental churches or that the Moslems bestow upon a sacred shrine. Little girls dressed in white stood upon either side as its guardians, while the voters marched to the polls with flags, flowers, and songs of triumph, and repeated cries of " Long live liberty! "

Although the people, even in local matters, were wholly unaccustomed to registering their will by vote or ballot, nevertheless the elections took place in all parts of the country without disturbance, and the successful candidates were sent upon their way to Constantinople with solemn and stately ceremony.

On December 17, 1908, parliament was opened by Sultan Hamid II, in a building he had put in readiness for the purpose in the old city of Stamboul upon the Square of Saint Sophia. The assembly was a motley gathering of Turks, Albanians, Koords, Syrians, Armenians, Greeks, Bulgarians, and Arabs, representatives of historic races hitherto regarded as more or less mutually hostile to each other, but now comprising the Chamber of Deputies for the Ottoman Empire, entrusted with the task of enacting measures that should establish and perpetuate the constitution. Ahmed Riza Pasha, himself recently returned from Paris, where he had been in exile because of his advanced ideas of liberty, was made President of the Chamber. It was well known that he had been from the first a leader in the Young Turk party and a man of unusual ability and integrity.

Among the populations of the country there was widespread and anxious doubt as to the ability of the party in power to unite the discordant and even hostile races into a harmonious whole that would be able safely to pilot the affairs of state through the turbulent seas that threatened. In the meantime it was evident, through repeated decrees and proclamations issued in the name of "The Committee," that far-seeing and able leaders, their names even unknown, were alert to the situation and ready with prompt firmness to meet emergencies. The large majority of the members of parliament were Moslems, while the Young Turk, or parliamentary, party held the reins of government. While Hamid II occupied the throne as sultan he did not under the constitution figure largely in the affairs of state. Although an *irade* for the constitution had been issued over his signature, he failed, at the opening of parliament, to reaffirm his allegiance to it or to take oath for its maintenance. This failure was noted by the constitutionalists in the body and freely discussed. There were few, if any, who were convinced that the sultan had met with any real change of heart in favor of a rep-

THE CONSTITUTION VINDICATED

resentative government, although he had at various times declared his belief in the new order.

Naturally a party arose in opposition to the party in power, and we soon began to hear of the Liberal Union party, which represented those who had little control of affairs but who desired to secure such control. The Constitutional party, or the Committee of Union and Progress, seemed to be confident of its ability to maintain control of the government through its hold upon the army, in which it seemed to have supreme confidence.

Through methods best known to himself, Sultan Abdul Hamid was able to enlist the service of the Liberal Unionists, and by their aid, with the assistance of Prince Burhan ed Din, his fourth son, and the lavish use of money among the troops, upon the 13th day of April, 1909, with little warning, the troops in the city shot or otherwise removed their officers who were known to be in sympathy with the party in power, took possession of the parliament building, killing several of the members, and drove from the city the leaders of the Young Turk party, who fled to save their lives.

It appeared to the outside world, as well as to the residents in Constantinople, that the new régime had terminated with its leaders in flight, Sultan Hamid in full possession of the government, and parliament too terrified to do anything even had it the power. Orders were sent at once to Cilicia, where for months trouble between Armenians and Moslems had been threatening, to kill the Armenians. Almost simultaneously at Adana, Tarsus, Mersin, Alexandretta, Kessab, and other places a general onslaught was made upon armed as well as defenseless Armenians, in which the police and soldiers took part, while the vali, or chief magistrate, made no effort to restrain them. This continued for three or four days, during which time in many places armed Armenians offered stiff resistance and many thousands of Armenians and not a few Turks lost their lives. Two American missionaries — Rev. D. Miner Rogers and Mr. Maurer — were shot while fighting fire in the mission seminary at Adana, which was at that time crowded with helpless and unarmed refugees. It transpired that at the same time similar instructions for an attack upon the Armenians were sent from the palace to other parts of Turkey, but happily only in Adana and vicinity did the local authorities acquiesce. There is also clear evidence that a similar onslaught upon Christians was arranged for the city of Constantinople, to begin on or about Saturday, the 24th of April.

In the meantime the leaders of the Young Turk party, who had fled for their lives from Constantinople, repaired by rail to Salonica, where they rallied, with marvelous skill and speed, an army of old recruits and hastily gathered volunteers and began at once to transport the same with full equipments by rail to the outskirts of Constantinople, so that by Saturday, the 24th, only eleven days from the date of the uprising in the capital, the forces at their command, within striking distance of the palace of Abdul Hamid, and in command of all the strategic position about the capital, were large enough to insure their taking possession of the person of the sultan at any time they chose. Upon Tuesday, the 27th of April, the Chamber of Deputies and the Senate, sitting as the National Assembly of the empire, met under the presidency of Said Pasha, to which body a proclamation by the Sheik-ul-Islam deposing Sultan Hamid II, upon the ground of misgovernment and of treason to the Moslem faith, was read, and upon which the Assembly took immediate

THE CONSTITUTION VINDICATED

and unanimous action. A delegation of four deputies at once proceeded to the palace and there informed the deposed sultan of his fate. That night he, with a few ladies of the harem and several servants, was put upon a special train, and at two o'clock on Wednesday morning, the 28th of April, he set out for Salonica, and within twenty-four hours was there confined in a villa under heavy guard, himself a prisoner in exile in two weeks from the day he captured the government at Constantinople and set out to annul constitutional government and stagger the world by a general slaughter of Armenians and other Christians throughout the length and breadth of his empire.

His brother, Reshad Effendi, himself a prisoner for thirty-three years, according to the laws and customs of Islam was made sultan as Mehmed V, who, upon taking office, proclaimed his allegiance to the constitution and revealed his liberal views regarding the principles that dominate the new order. A liberal cabinet was at once formed and the newly organized government set out with vigor to restore order both in the capital and in the provinces. Under martial law in Constantinople those guilty of treason and mutiny in the recent uprising against the constitution were executed, and a court martial was appointed to inquire into the cause of the massacres in Cilicia and to punish the guilty parties. The commander of the constitutional forces, General Shevket, himself an Arab from Bagdad, showed great military as well as diplomatic ability in his masterly power to manage and control his quickly organized forces, but he refused to accept any civil office under the new government.

Within a surprisingly brief period the provinces became quiet and mutual confidence was restored. The conflict had been brief but desperate, the deposed sultan striking to regain the prestige he had lost under the constitution and through the supremacy of the Young Turk party, while the party itself and the interests represented by parliament were convinced that upon the success of their resistance depended the future freedom of the country. After the few brief days of desperate action victory perched upon the banner of constitutional and orderly government, and there is reason to expect that government by massacre has become in Turkey a thing of the past.

In the ten months which have transpired since the promulgation of the constitution it has been clearly demonstrated that the enlightened people of the empire are in favor of the new régime, although there is great and wide-spread ignorance as to the real meaning of liberty and the actual benefits the new order will bring to the country.

When for a brief period it seemed that Abdul Hamid had again secured control of affairs at Constantinople, a leading Moslem paper of the capital published an open letter to the sultan warning him that the constitution and parliament must not be tampered with, and he made haste to declare that he intended to champion both. Probably the most difficult breach to bridge over is that which separates between the Armenian revolutionists and the fanatical Mohammedans. These Armenians seem bound not to forget that they occupied that country long before the Turks came into power, while the Moslems cannot blot from their memory the various race conflicts that have taken place during the last century and the superior capacity exhibited by the Armenians for commercial, industrial, and intellectual advance. Revolutionary agita-

THE CONSTITUTION VINDICATED

tion upon the part even of the few cannot but bring harm to the Armenians as a race and make more difficult the application of the principles of fraternity upon which the constitution is established.

Constitutional and orderly government is not yet completely established throughout the Ottoman Empire. It goes without saying that the spies who have lost their salaries and the palace camarilla who have been cast out of office are not especially cordial to any government that proposes to be directed by law and order. Throughout the interior in all the educational centers Ottoman clubs or clubs of Unity and Progress have been formed for the purpose of studying the principles of good government, what it promises to the governed, and what it rightfully can expect from its subjects. In these clubs Christians and Moslems meet upon equal footing and, in cases not a few, the leading minds of the executive committees are professors in the American colleges. The missionaries have repeatedly been invited to address these clubs upon national, intellectual, social, and religious topics, and the spirit shown throughout the country has been most promising.

The policy of government employed by Abdul Hamid has been openly and officially repudiated. The rapidity and effectiveness with which his seizure of the government was met, his own deposition, and the extreme punishment meted out to his agents in the endeavor to reestablish his authority and to restore the old order, all show plainly that the party in power will admit of no absolutism upon the part of the reigning sultan. Mehmed V, the new sultan, understanding this, has already revealed his purpose to exercise his authority through and by the will of the people. It has also been made clear that, whereas in other days the people possessed few rights that the sultan upon the throne was expected to respect and with no voice in the affairs of government, now they speak with a force that even the throne must recognize. It is of no little significance that Sultan Hamid was deposed, after the declaration of the Sheik-ul-Islam, by the unanimous vote of the House of Parliament and the Senate in joint session. Parliament represented the people. This is a privilege and a power that the people of Turkey will not easily abandon.

It is evident that the Moslems are laboring under the conviction that the new order guarantees to them liberty of conscience in matters of religion. This attitude is manifest throughout the country, but with different degrees of demonstration. Mixed gatherings of Christians and Moslems addressed by well-recognized Christian leaders upon religious topics, Moslem and non-Moslem pupils studying side by side in Christian schools, close and fraternal cooperation in various Ottoman clubs, all point to the fact that a new era in religious liberty has dawned upon the empire.

Much has been said by the leaders in the new régime in approbation of American institutions in the country and the preparative work they have done in training the young for self-government, and in preparing the masses of the people for the right use and appreciation of a larger liberty. Probably none of the prominent leaders in the New Turk party received this training in American schools. And yet it is evident that the atmosphere of these institutions of higher learning has, in a greater or less degree, permeated the land, influencing hundreds and thousands who have never been enrolled as pupils. Enver Bey, the young organizer and leader of the Young Turk party, expressed this when he declared to the president of one of the American mission colleges that they would not have dared undertake the reform at this time had they not trusted to the work accomplished during the last half-century by the large number of American institutions scattered throughout the country.

The changes in Turkey are not only political, but they indicate a marked advance movement in Mohammedanism. This fact was clearly recognized by Abdul Hamid II, who, in his desperate attempt in April to regain his lost power, appealed to the fanaticism of the old Turks by the declaration that the new party was tampering with the sacred and time-honored laws of their religion. The declaration of the soldiers in Constantinople as they shot their officers and intimidated parliament was that they were fighting to restore to its proper place in the government the sacred law of Islam.

It is unquestionably startling to the Mohammedan of the old school to be informed that the Christian has equal rights with himself before the law and that there is any possibility of the two being in any sense of the word "brethren." It is certainly a new Islam that permits the Mohammedan freely to read religious books other than of his own faith and to put his children into Christian schools. "Liberty" applied to matters pertaining to religion is putting a new and untried meaning to an old and almost unknown word. The highest authority in Islam has officially declared that Moslems have no right to call Christians "infidels," and a proclamation issued to the Christians in Macedonia by the Young Turk party, and over their official seal, calls them "brethren," and declares that Christians and Moslems are worshipers of the same God and Father, and therefore members of the same family.

DAYBREAK IN TURKEY

The new dawn that has come to the Turkish Empire indicates the breaking of a new political, intellectual, social, and religious day. Much time must transpire ere the sun of this new day shall reach the high noon of its power and glory. At times mists must obscure its vision and great black clouds of threatening storm may sweep in blinding fury across its face. And still higher and yet higher must it mount into the heavens, until at last its far-extending rays shall send down into every dark corner of Albania, Koordistan, Armenia, Mesopotamia, and Arabia, as well as the more immediate portions of that great empire, the warmth and glow and life-giving vigor of the full-orbed day. The daybreak has come, and the day in all its glory must follow.

INDEX

INDEX

ADEN, 133.
Adrianople, 33, 173.
Agriculture, methods, 23, 233; products, 23, 24.
Aintab, 139, 171; medical work, 208.
Albanians, 78, 80, 261; work among, 262.
American Bible Society, 154.
American Board of Commissioners for Foreign Missions, 90, 145, 146.
American College for Girls, 189.
Amurath I, 1359–1403, 33.
Anatolia College, 191, 234.
Anderson, Sec. Rufus, 123, 171, 183.
Angell, James B., quotation, 136.
Arabia, missions in, 132.
Armenia, traditional history, 65; political history, 66; population, 67; religious history, 68.
Armenian Church, Evangelical; *see* Evangelical Armenian Church.
Armenian Church, Gregorian; *see* Gregorian Church.
Armenian Evangelical Union, 163.
Armenians, 65–70; tour among, 123–126; interest in, 144, 149; desire for political freedom, 269.
Army, organization of, 43.

BAJAZET I, 33.
Barnum, H. N., 186, 216.
Barton, George A., quotation, 118.
Beach, Harlan P., quotation, 180.
Bebek, boys' school, 164, 171; seminary, 182.
Beirut, 122, 137; medical work, 208; press, 199; school, 184; Syrian Protestant College, 187, 190.
Bible, Armenian, 150–153, 198; publication, 153; translations, 199.
Biblical interest in Turkey, 19.
Bird, Mr., 123.
Bithynia Union, 228.

Black stone of the Kaaba, 96.
Bliss, Daniel, 187.
Bliss, Edwin Munsell, quotation, 222.
British and Foreign Bible Society, 151, 154.
Bryce, Hon. James, quotation, 196.
Bulgarians, 80; in Macedonia, 263; work among, 173.

CABINET, Turkish, changes in, 283.
"Capitulations," 241.
Central Turkey College, Aintab, 189.
Church Missionary Society, 145.
Cilicia Union, 228.
Circassians, 80.
Classical interest in Turkey, 18.
Colleges, official recognition, 189; present need, 286.
Committee of Ottoman Union and Progress, 279.
Concessions, 241.
Constantinople, 137; missionary center, 87, 93–97.
Constitutional government, present problems, 285.
Constitutional liberty granted, 281.
Cromer, Lord, quotation, 10, 40, 50, 112.
Crusades, 54, 59.
Cyprus, possession by England, 47.

DARAZI, founder of Druses, 55.
Death penalty for Mohammedan convert, 133, 250.
Decline of Empire, 15.
Dennis, James S., quotation, 206, 260, 274.
De Redcliffe, Sir Stratford, 250, 253.
Diarbekr, 128, 130, 139.
Dionysius, 160.
Disciples of Christ, 145.
Dodge, Dr. Asa, 207.
Druses, 55, 78.

[303]

INDEX

Dunmore, Rev. and Mrs., 130.
Dwight, H. G. O., tour in Asia Minor, 123–126.
Dwight, Henry Otis, quotation, 92.

EDICT of Toleration, 1453, 241.
Education, 106, 181; of priests, 106, 159, 160; of women, 107, 187; Lancasterian schools, 160; theological, 176; Turkish, 193; industrial, 234.
Emigration, 236.
England, first treaty relations with Turkey, 34; seizure of Cyprus, 47; policy in Turkey, 48.
English taught in schools, 183, 184.
Erzerum, 127, 139.
Eski-Zagra, 173.
Euphrates College, Harpoot, 186, 188, 190, 191, 229.
Evangelical Armenian Church, 161, 165, 166, 167, 168, 174, 177.

FATALISM, 210.
Financial condition, 271.
First Turkish ambassador, 33.
Fisk, Pliny, 87, 119, 120, 121, 145, 149.
Free Church of Scotland, 54.

GERMANY, policy in Turkey, 48; influence in Turkey, 270.
Goodell, William, 121, 123, 157, 159, 174, 177, 198, 249.
Grant, Dr. Asahel, 127, 129, 207.
Greco-Turkish war, 121, 123.
Greek Church, 59–62.
Greeks, work among, 143; in Macedonia, 264.
Gregorian (Armenian) Church, 68–70; deterioration, 70, 79, 102, 104; jealousy in, 102; political organization, 105; reform in, 150, 165, 237.

HAGOPOS, 163.
Haig, father of Armenian race, 65.
Hall of the Holy Garment, 96.
Hamid II. *see* Sultan Abdul Hamid II.

Hamlin, Cyrus, 164, 182, 234.
Harem, 41.
Harpoot, 131; educational work, 186; printing-press, 201.
Harpoot Evangelical Union, 228, 229.
"Hatti Sherif of Gul Hane," granting of religious liberty, 250.
Health of missionary, 122.
Hejaz, 133.
Hepworth, George H., 216; quotation, 212.
Historical interest in Turkey, 17.
Holmes, Mr., 128.
Hospitals, self-support in, 209, 227, 228.

INDUSTRIAL education, 234.
Industrial reform, 233.
Imperial Protestant Charter of 1850, 252.
Islam, Koran, 35, 201; death penalty for change of faith, 133, 250; fatalism, 210.

JACOBITES, 57–59.
Janissaries, 32.
Jerusalem, 122.
Jesuit schools, 183.
Jews, 56, 57; revival of interest in, 86; work among, 140, 143.

KAABA, 95.
Keith-Falconer Mission in Arabia, 133.
King, Jonas, 120, 121, 160.
Koordistan Missionary Society, 229.
Koords, history, 73; character, 74; armed by government, 75; religion, 76, 78.
Koran, 201; basis of law, 35.

LANCASTER, Joseph, 160.
Lancasterian schools, 181.
Lawrence, Edward A., quotation, 14, 64.
Laws, founded on Koran, 35.

MACEDONIA, Turkish rule in, 261, 263; uprising in, 264, 276, 279; reforms promised, 275; Young

[304]

INDEX

Turk Party in, 279; constitution restored, 281.
Mahomet I, 1413–1421, 33.
Mahomet II, conqueror of Greek Empire, 33.
Marash, 172, 188.
Maronites, 54.
Martyn, Henry, 124.
Massacres, 218.
Mecca, 94.
Medical missionaries, 207.
Medina, 207.
"Memoirs of William Goodell," quotation, 232.
Methodist Episcopal Board (U. S.), 146.
Midhat Pasha, 281.
Mineral resources, 24.
Mission policy, 119, 139, 141, 157, 159, 162, 207, 223.
Missionaries, moral influence of, 142; noted, 177; contribution to knowledge of country, 115; to literature, 199; to industry, 233; trust in, 216; relief work, 218; relation to native churches, 175; under English protection, 241; charges against, 255.
Missionary interest, awakening of, 86.
Missions, division of field, 145; problems of, 115; object of, 108.
"Mohammedan World of To-day," quotation, 72, 248, 266.
Mohammedans, contact with Christianity, 113–115, 119, 238; interest in, 144; converts, 254, 257; religious liberty promised, 250; no religious liberty, 255.
"Multeka," code of laws, 35.

NATIVE CHURCH, self-support, 224–227; self-propagation, 228.
New Turk Party, 79, 268, 279.
Nicholas, Czar, epithet applied to, 15.
Norton, Thomas H., quotation, 170.
Nusairiyeh, 53.

ORCHAN, 32.
Orphans, industrial training of, 234.
Osman, founder of dynasty, 31.

PALESTINE, missionaries to, 86.
Parker, John M., 138.
Parsons, Levi, 86, 87, 119, 120, 145, 149.
Pashtimaljian school, 160, 181.
Patriarch, Greek, 60; Gregorian, 69; power of, 105.
Periodical publications, 200.
Perkins, Mr., 126.
Persecution of "Evangelicals," 166.
Peters, John P., quotation, 156.
Philippopolis, 173.
Physicians, native, 208.
Pomeroy, Dr., 167.
Population of Turkey, 16.
"Porte, The," meaning of, 34.
Postal system, 26.
Presbyterian Board of Missions, 146; work among Maronites, 54.
Press, printing, 172, 197; freedom guaranteed, 282.
Priests, Christian, low standard of, 103.
Privy council, 36.
Property, right to hold, 244.
Protestant Charter of 1847, 252.

RAILROADS, 24, 25, 47.
Ramsay, W. M., quotation, 240.
Reformed Church, 145.
Reformed (Dutch) Church of America, in Arabia, 133.
Reforms in Gregorian Church, 237.
Religious liberty granted, 250, 253.
"Researches in Armenia," Smith and Dwight, 123–126.
Revolutionary parties, 264, 270.
Riggs, Elias, 198.
Roadways, 24.
Robert College, 184, 185, 189, 191.
Roman Catholics, opposition of, 121, 144, 162.
Russell, Earl, 255.
Russia, opposition to missionary work, 182; influence in Turkey, 268, 270.
Russian Bible Society, 150–152.

ST. GREGORY the Illuminator, 68.
St. Paul's Institute, Tarsus, 189.

INDEX

Salonica, 140.
Samakov, Collegiate and Theological Institute, 187.
Schauffler, Dr., 143, 182.
Schneider, Dr., 171.
Schools, present need of, 286.
Self-support, hospitals, 209, 227; church, 224, 228; schools, 226, 228.
Selim III, 1789–1807, reforms of, 85.
Seventh Day Adventists, 145.
Sheik-ul-Islam, 35, 282.
Size of Territory, 16.
Smith, Eli, tour in Asia Minor, 123–126.
Smyrna, 137, 140, 172.
Spies, government, 227; abolished, 282.
"Sublime Porte," 34.
Suliman "the great," 1520–1566, 34.
Sultan Adbul Aziz, 255.
Sultan Abdul Hamid II, succession to throne, 41; character, 41, 46, 48, 270; absolute power in government, 35, 43; in religion, 46, 93, 94, 96; foreign relations, 47; attempt to subdue Koords, 75; system of espionage, 277; fear of Young Turks, 278; restores constitution to Macedonia, 281.
Sultan Abdul Medjid, 250, 251; grants religious liberty, 253.
Syrian Church, 57–59.
Syrian Protestant College, 187, 190.
Syrians, work among, 121, 144, 173.

Tamerlane, 32, 33.
Taxation, system of, 51, 279.
Telegraphy, 26, 234.
Territory, population, 16; size, 16.
Theological schools, 190.

Townsend, Meredith, quotation, 22, 30, 100.
Transportation, 25.
"Travels and Researches in Asia Minor," 138.
Treaty of Berlin, 256.
Treaty of Paris, 253.
Treaty rights, 243.
Trebizond, 127, 139.
"Turk," religious significance, 77.
Turkey, importance as mission field, 89; relations with foreign powers, 241; policy of suppression, 268.
Turkish schools, 193.
Turkomen, 80.
Turks, origin, 31, 77; character, 79; dominance over non-Moslems, 78, 81.

Unions of native churches, 176.
United Free Church of Scotland, in Arabia, 133.
United States, Armenians in, 236.
United States, relations with Turkish government, 34, 45, 241, 245.

Vali, power of, 36.
Vartenes, expelled from church, 165.
Vilayet, 36.

Ward, William Hayes, quotation, 148.
Wheeler, Crosby H., 185, 201, 224.
Williams, Talcott, quotation, 274.

Yemen, 133.
Young Turk Party, 278; in Macedonia, 279.

Zwemer, S. M., quotation, 84.